THE BELFAST BLITZ

THE BELFAST BLITZ

Luftwaffe Raids in Northern Ireland, 1941

SEAN McMAHON

Sean McMahon

THE BREHON PRESS
BELFAST

Published by
The Brehon Press Ltd,
19 Glen Crescent
Belfast BT11 9NJ
Northern Ireland

© 2010 Sean McMahon

ISBN: 978 1 905474 31 8

Printed and bound by JF Print, Sparkford, Yeovil

CONTENTS

For Paddy O'Carolan, who remembers it

ACKNOWLEDGEMENTS

I would like to thank those who were generous with time, advice and help: the staff of the Central Library in Derry, especially Jane Nicholas and Gerry Quinn, the staff of the Linen Hall Library of Belfast, especially John Killen, Maeve Breslin, Richard Doherty, Garbhán Downey, Brian McMahon, and, most of all, Paddy O'Carolan. And finally, a special thanks to Paul Carson at the *Belfast Telegraph* photo library for kindly giving permission to reproduce the images featured in the picture section.

1

Rumours of War

THE SECOND DECADE OF THE LIFE of the Northern Ireland state was known justly as the Hungry Thirties. Belfast, depending on the heavy industries of shipbuilding, engineering, flax-spinning, rope-making, was particularly affected by the world slump that followed the Wall Street stock-market crash of October 1929. Unemployment soared in the years that followed, reaching 50,000 in 1932. That year saw an unheard-of phenomenon – non-sectarian riots. They were based essentially on the lowest but most powerful element in urban economics, absolute hunger. Unemployment affected 36 percent of the population, a majority of them Catholics, for the usual reasons, and when their entitlement to the dole ran out they were forced to suffer the ignominy of relying on outdoor relief. This pitiful allowance in Belfast (for husband, wife and one child) came to twelve shillings (60 pence in modern terms but because of lower prices able to buy more then), half the rate of Manchester. If any client remained on the list for a year the relief stopped and the only alternatives were hunger or the hated workhouse. The scheme was administered by the Board of Guardians, the chief concern of which was the comfort of the ratepayers rather than the welfare of the unemployed.

The chairman, Lily Coleman, received a lot of public complaint when she remarked that if Catholics made the same effort at finding work as they did under the blankets there would be less of a problem. Though hers is the name that is still execrated in Catholic areas she certainly spoke for the greater majority of the guardians. One of her colleagues complained that 60 percent of the applicants for relief 'were Roman Catholics from one part of the city' not realising how self-condemnatory his remarks were. The riots of October had the usual intensity for which the city remains famous but this time Orange and Green combined against the mean-spirited public officials so that the alarmed government, newly installed in palatial Stormont, brought pressure on the board to improve their provision of relief. The détente did not last; the government, using the Orange Order, of which almost all the cabinet were vociferous members, soon sowed the seeds of sectarian hatred successfully again though it was clear that they feared communists like Betty Sinclair more than the disorganised and generally apolitical Catholics.

The visit of the well-meaning if politically insensitive George V as part of his silver jubilee celebrations in 1935 gave the impetus for old-style sectarian rioting. There were violent rumblings in May during and after the royal visit, and as the Twelfth approached, even Sir Richard Dawson Bates (1876–1949), the steely Minister of Home Affairs, did the unmentionable and banned Orange marches that summer. Sir Joseph Davison, the Orange Grand Master, responded with the not unexpected statement: 'You may be certain that on the Twelfth of July the Orangemen will be marching throughout Northern Ireland.' Bates immediately rescinded the ban and in the riots that followed nine people were killed and 2,241 Catholics were driven from their homes in the York Street area and in the 'Village', the Protestant enclave between Tates Avenue and the Donegall Road. Many settled in a development at Glenard, later incorporated into Ardoyne, thus changing the demographic and political weighting of the area and making it no longer a safe Unionist seat.

I have deliberately adverted to that aspect of the Thirties that saw the recrudescence of the old hatreds because of a temporary lull in mutual animosity during the war and especially the period of the air raids. The Luftwaffe was oddly undiscriminating in its attacks and Shankill Road women and children found themselves companionably sharing the deep cellars of Clonard monastery with Falls Road 'Fenians'. Truly, as Trinculo remarks in *The Tempest*: 'Misery acquaints a man with strange bedfellows.' The time of these raids was six years into the future. The increase of sectarian tension at this time of the worst violence for many years was to have a mixture of effects as the possibility of war became a probability. There arose the problem of that loaded word 'loyalty' that tended to be bandied about by Unionist politicians. In March 1938 the Stormont parliament assured Neville Chamberlain (1869–1940), the British prime minister, that he could 'confidently rely upon the people of Ulster to share the responsibilities and burdens with their kith and kin in other parts of the United Kingdom and the Empire to the utmost of her resources'. The spur for this declaration was the Nazi Anschluss of Austria and the beginning of German demands for the lost Sudeten lands, assigned to Czechoslovakia at the end of the Great War. Behind the use of the word loyalty there was the unstated but understood assumption that the loyalty of the Catholic quarter of the city's population could not be guaranteed.

An even more potent motive for the government's public utterance of unwavering allegiance was the need to respond to de Valera's 1937 constitution that took the newly named Éire out of the British Empire. Two things were becoming clear: war with Germany was a moral certainty and during it Éire would remain neutral. Britain was not ready for war. Both Stanley Baldwin (1867–1947) and Neville Chamberlain, who followed him as prime minister, with clear memories of twenty years earlier, refusing to consider the possibility of another cataclysmic world conflict, had done little in the way of rearmament, in spite of repeated warnings from Winston Churchill (1874–1965) of Germany's intentions. Rearmament began sluggishly at first and then more rapidly as the pace of events in Europe accelerated. A war economy held promises of increased employment for the 101,967 people who were unemployed in 1935, then 23.3 percent of the total in the city. The Catholic population of Belfast, according to the 1937 figures, stood at 104,372, 23.8 percent of the total of 438,086, and were a large majority of the workless, and *a fortiori* of the 36 percent of the population who lived below the poverty line. (These latter were later to be referred to in many statements made during the war, with some mathematical inaccuracy, as the 'submerged tenth'.) Whatever about matters of loyalty or patriotism the prospect of employment reconciled many to the coming struggle. Some men from west Belfast were to find their first work as adults helping to clear up the debris after the raids.

The ailing shipbuilding industry, mainly the firms of Harland & Wolff and Workman Clark (the 'wee yard'), received a great boost in war orders, turning out between September 1939 and the end of the war a total of 170 warships, mainly destroyers and corvettes, including HMS *Belfast*, and the aircraft carrier HMS *Formidable*. The full list of the 140 ships built in the Island, as the site of the main shipyards was known, between 1940 and 1944, included six aircraft carriers, three cruisers and two depot ships (intended to be mobile supply bases); the rest were corvettes, minesweepers and frigates. Originally Dargan's Island, created from the residue of the railway king's excavations, it had been in the mid-nineteenth-century an urban pleasure resort but was closed to accommodate the shipbuilders. The firm also turned out 123 merchant carriers – 10 percent of the total UK output. Three thousand ships damaged at sea in the Atlantic convoys were refurbished in the dry docks with up to 100 vessels finding berths at any one time. The threat of war and the organisation of the city's industries to meet the needs of the coming conflict lowered the numbers of the unemployed to 92,000 in 1938, still only a two percent decrease.

The newest industry was plane making, begun in 1936 on reclaimed land at Sydenham beside the new Belfast airport where

Short Brothers of Rochester were encouraged by the government to combine with Harland & Wolff to build aeroplanes. The new firm was labelled Short Brothers and Harland but for verbal economy became universally known simply as Shorts. Eventually the firm employed 20,000 people at the Sydenham works and at Newtownards, where flying trials were initiated.

Shorts at the beginning of the enterprise made small Hereford bombers and air transports called Bristol Bombays but it was decided that their contribution to the war effort, as this greatest of all priorities become known, should preferably be Stirling bombers and the stately Sunderland flying-boats, not inappropriate for the loughside works. By the end of a year and a half of declared war, Shorts had built 206 aircraft and had been given the title of 'the finest seaplane-manufacturing base in the British Isles'. In all, the factory produced 238 Stirlings and 133 Sunderlands, and twenty million aircraft parts. Harland & Wolff, as well as building both warships and merchant vessels, and repairing and converting the 3,000 ships, diversified into other armaments. They built a total of 550 tanks at Carrickfergus, including the Churchill, which was designed in Belfast, and many individual pieces of ordnance in the yards sited in Queen's Island. These included by 1943 more than 10,000 munitions items and 801 mountings for guns. Other munitions works in Counties Antrim and Down produced seventy-five million shells, 180 million incendiary bullets and 50,000 bayonets. In this way the two complexes were able to employ more than 30,000 people and thereby give a healthier look to the unemployment statistics.

Other traditional industries were adapted to serve the wartime needs. Mackie's foundry on the Springfield Road, equipped with modern machinery, became a main source of shells for the famous Swedish light artillery gun, the Bofors. Sirocco Engineering, the leading manufacturer of heating systems, supplied heat and ventilation plant for underground munitions works in Britain. The linen mills made their contribution with casings and linings, especially of plane wings and bodies, providing 200 million yards of cloth, and the Royal Navy used as much cordage as the Belfast Rope Works could supply. Their output was one third of the total for the whole of the UK, amounting to a quarter of a million tons. They were also responsible for 50,000 camouflage and cargo nets. Derry, already groomed as the port of rescue and repair for Western Approaches, was also the main source of shirts and battledresses for the armed forces. They produced 90 percent of the shirts the armed forces used (including bush shirts for the North African campaign) and the shirts that were part of the complete set of clothing presented to servicemen on their demobilisation.

There was a curious mindset in Northern Ireland rather like 'doublethink', as described by George Orwell (1903–57) in his novel *Nineteen Eighty-Four* (1949). The people were delighted with the increased employment and probably realised, if they thought about it, that with so much of the work being devoted to weapons of war the factories, airfields and docks must become targets should war break out. At the same time they had convinced themselves that Northern Ireland in its remote isolation would never be a target of attack from the air. Government warnings had made it clear that hostilities would not be likely to stop at the coast of continental Europe, as they had in the Great War. Still they believed that though a war would mean shortages – even privation – it surely would not entail death or destruction, at least not on Irish soil. They began to breathe more easily when Chamberlain arrived back from Munich with, as he said at Croydon airport, 'a piece of paper' signed by Adolf Hitler (1889–1945), the head of Nazi Germany, Édouard Deladier (1884–1970), Premier of France, Benito Mussolini (1883–1945), self-styled '*Il Duce*' of Italy, and himself, that assured the world that Germany had no further territorial demands once the German-speaking mountainous area of western Czechoslovakia, known as Sudetenland, tacked on to Czech territory by the ultimately farcical Treaty of Versailles (28 June 1919), had been returned to the

Heimatland. Both Deladier and Chamberlain were anxious to preserve peace for as long as possible, remembering the horrors of the earlier conflict. They were dubbed 'appeasers' by those who claimed that Hitler's intention was world denomination; the phrase *'Morgen, die ganze Welt'* ('Tomorrow, the whole world') was used freely in Nazi rhetoric.

Neither of the anti-Fascist leaders really believed that the Sudetenland would satisfy *Der Führer* but were in no position to make a stand over that particular piece of territory. France was proud of its Maginot Line, a strip of fortifications stretching from the Swiss border to Belgium, built between Germany and France to defend the territories of Alsace and Lorraine ceded to France in 1919. It was a substantial defence system but ultimately irrelevant since France was invaded through undefended Belgium in 1940. Britain had deliberately not rearmed and relied on the English Channel as its line of defence. Chamberlain, already ill with the cancer that killed him two years later, was consciously or otherwise playing for time and may have even hoped that there might be some truth in his words broadcast from Downing Street on 30 September 1938: 'This is the second time in our history that there has come back from Germany to Downing Street peace with honour. I believe it is peace in our time.' The phrase 'peace with honour' had already been used to good effect by Benjamin Disraeli (1804–81), returning from the Congress of Berlin on 16 July 1878, and even earlier by Lord John Russell (1792–1878) in 1853, but those men had spoken with the confidence of leaders of a growing and not ailing empire. Chamberlain knew that as he waved the 'piece of paper' not a single RAF airfield had any Spitfires, the main cause of Britain's winning the Battle of Britain in the summer of 1940 and of at least postponing the invasion of Britain. When, however, Germany occupied the rest of Czechoslovakia the following March it was clear that war was inevitable.

For Nazi Germany the real enemies, the only nations capable of preventing its manifest destiny of world supremacy, were the US and the USSR, mainly because of their natural resources. Britain and France, in spite of their illustrious pasts, were essentially side issues, merely stepping stones in the causeway that would lead to the Master Race's dream of global suzerainty. It was a piece of supreme cynicism on the part of both men when, on 23 August 1939, Hitler and Josef Stalin (1879–1953), the Russian supremo, made through their foreign ministers, the Molotov–Ribbentrop non-aggression pact, under which they agreed each to remain neutral and to refrain from acts of aggression against each other if either went to war. Some unpublished clauses in the agreement concerned the sharing of Poland between their two countries, Germany to take the western part while East Poland was incorporated into the USSR. It was the next step in Hitler's grand strategy and Stalin, absolutely convinced of a future German invasion, used the two years left to him to make what preparations he could to defend Russia. He, too, had cosmic ambitions to bring about the Marxist imperative of world domination. Chamberlain and Daladier had reassured Poland of intervention should Germany invade, which it did on 1 September 1939. The Second World War was about to begin.

2

Out of Range?

AT 11.15AM ON SUNDAY, 3 SEPTEMBER 1939, the slightly quavering voice of Chamberlain was heard on all the wirelesses, as they were called then, speaking to the intent listeners:

> This morning, the British Ambassador in Berlin handed the German government a final Note stating that, unless we heard from them by eleven o'clock that they were prepared at once to withdraw their troops from Poland, a state of war would exist between us. I have to tell you now that no such undertaking has been received, and that consequently this country is at war with Germany.

It was notably different from his speech at the end of September the year before when he promised 'peace for our time'. Almost immediately the banshee wail of the air-raid sirens – a false alarm as it turned out – seemed to confirm that this time it was going to be war for our time. Little more than eleven months separated the two Downing Street announcements and in Britain at least there was a kind of terror-stricken relief that the disgrace of the Munich Agreement that had handed Czechoslovakia over to the Nazis (total occupation was completed in March 1939) had been exorcised by the refusal to countenance the invasion of Poland.

Britain – and that effectively included Northern Ireland – was not well prepared for hostilities and one of the remarks of Stanley Baldwin, who had been prime minister before Chamberlain, had become even more telling: 'The bomber will always get through.' Northern Ireland, firm in its belief that it was out of range of Luftwaffe bombers, took the news of the declaration of war without notable hysteria. This insouciance was general: Lady Londonderry, who had earlier opined to Sir Samuel Hoare (1880–1959), Chamberlain's Home Secretary, that Viscount Craigavon (1871–1940), the Unionist prime minister, was 'ga-ga', wrote to her husband early in September 1939 to say: 'All sorts of rot are going on here. Air-raid warnings and blackouts. As if anyone cared or wished to bomb Belfast!' Both the British High Command and the Westminster cabinet seemed to agree. General Sir Hastings Ismay (1887–1965), later Churchill's Chief-of-Staff, considered that there was very little likelihood of any attack being made and Charles Markbreiter, Assistant Secretary at the Home Office, told Sir Wilfred Spender that 'the position of Northern Ireland was so sheltered that he did not think we need worry very much about war measures'.

Edmund Warnock (1887–1971), private personal secretary to Bates in Home Affairs – who would later dismay John [Clarke] MacDermott (1896–1979), appointed Minister of Home Security in 1940, by refusing an offer of essential fire-fighting equipment because he was certain that even the east of the province lay beyond the range of the Luftwaffe's capacity to strike – assured the cabinet in the first months of the war that since Belfast was the most distant city of the UK from any possible enemy base, 'it is possible that we might escape attack altogether'. His argument was based mainly on distance: 'An attack on Northern Ireland would involve a flight of over 1,000 miles' and any force would 'twice have to pass through the active gun, searchlight and aeroplane defences of Great Britain.' MacDermott, who had been Unionist MP for Queen's, and later Lord Chief Justice (1951–71) of Northern Ireland, was younger, more vigorous and considerably more intelligent than his cabinet colleagues and was one of the few who understood the real nature of the threat. His brief that he carried out steadfastly in spite of lack of cooperation and even hostility from conservative colleagues was: 'public security, civil defence, the preservation of the peace and maintenance of order, the coordination of civil defence services and the protection of persons and property from injury or damage in the present emergency'. He did not succeed in carrying out these functions for a multiplicity of reasons but the chaos resulting from the Easter Week raids would have been infinitely worse without his work.

It was still a very divided community and Catholics/nationalists may not have been wholly behind Craigavon when he announced in a broadcast in February 1940, 'We are King's men and we shall be with you to the end.' He had urged the British government nearly a year before, in April 1939, to impose on Northern Ireland the same conscription that was in place in Britain. It caused the same uproar that had resulted from a similar proposal made in 1917. Eamon de Valera (1882–1974), then in his seventh year as Taoiseach of the country he had caused to be named as Éire two years earlier, and still with eight years of uninterrupted office to serve, called it 'an act of war against our nation'. Cardinal Joseph MacRory (1861–1945), speaking as Archbishop of Armagh and as such Primate of All Ireland, gave the opinion that resistance to such a move would be morally justified. (He had been Bishop of Down and Connor during the sectarian violence that accompanied the founding of the Northern Ireland state and had remained a severe critic of the Stormont government.)

The urge for inclusion was a typical demonstration of Unionist solidarity made with the absolute, not to say ruthless, sincerity so typical of Craigavon. It proved awkward for Chamberlain who did not want any kind of verbal civil war on his doorstop and he had to ask for no repetition of the demand: 'It will only be an embarrassment.' There was no objection, however, to volunteer enlistment and for the first six months of the war recruitment ran at 2,500 a month. By the spring of 1940 the rate of enlistment had fallen to less than half that figure. In fact the total number of volunteers from Northern Ireland from 1939 to 1945 was around 30,664, a figure that was remarkably close to the 28,774 from the south. The need, as it seemed to the wartime coalition government, to find more recruits brought back the question of conscription in Northern Ireland in the spring of 1941 when Britain's fortunes were at their lowest, though the decision of Adolf Hitler (1889–1945), the Nazi leader, to invade Russia that summer was a significant factor in Germany's final defeat.

Between Craigavon's first suggestion and the final decision by Winston Churchill, prime minister from May 1940, on 27 May not to impose conscription as 'more trouble than it was worth', there were two other attempts, by Craigavon again when Churchill became prime minister, and by Sir Wilfred Spender (1876–1960), the founder of the B-Specials and head of the Northern Ireland civil service, in November 1940. Both suggestions were again turned down by Churchill. A further attempt was made in 1942 by Warnock and again by Sir Basil Brooke (1888–1973) when he replaced as prime minister the disgraced John Miller Andrews (1871–1956) who was forced to resign in April 1943. The British War cabinet said no to all such offers for the best of reasons, 'more trouble than worth' being the main cause. The police had continually warned against it as unenforceable and there was a real fear that should it be imposed recruitment from Éire would immediately cease. There was a considerable gap between the show of loyalty that such suggestions implied and the general temper of the population. In fact the only 'conscripts' in the north were the members of the Territorial Army, the 'weekend soldiers' who were de facto members of the military from the moment they accepted their uniforms and began their training. Most had become members of the Royal Artillery and the gunners of the 24th and 25th batteries, recruited in Derry, played no part in home defence but with customary military logic were sent (by a long sea route to avoid U-Boats) to Egypt in November 1939.

The official drive for recruitment may have been stimulated by a sense of government guilt. Northern Ireland was singularly unprepared for modern war and Belfast, with the greatest concentration of population, was an obvious target. Neither Craigavon nor Andrews who succeeded him on the former's death on 24 November 1940 was capable of playing a role even in a defensive war. The cabinet was much as it had been since the state was founded in 1921. The members were hard-working and, allowing for the burden of the sectarianism that they all seemed to carry, honest. Their virtues as 'safe pairs of hands' were what the Unionist state needed to survive in its early days but they were unsuited to world wars. Unimaginative, they were convinced that the German bombers could never reach Ireland and so felt no urgent need to protect the population. Any 'unnecessary' expenditure was anathema to their provincial sense of fiscal probity. Air Raid Precautions, known 'for the duration', to use a phrase becoming ever more common, as ARP, in Belfast had fallen greatly behind the preparations made for comparative cities like Manchester and Birmingham. This dereliction was not entirely Stormont's fault. Craigavon was too ill to give any leadership and his most senior colleagues, Andrews and Bates, were temperamentally unsuited to dealing with the situation. The latter had become quite incoherent and could give no precise directions on policy. Spender, the cabinet Secretary, believed Bates to have been regularly drunk at his desk and his response to army communications about Belfast's vulnerability to air attack was simply a refusal to answer them. Westminster inevitably became more concerned with its own British affairs and taking Stormont's apparent lack of concern as policy proved reluctant to provide the necessary finance to implement the minimum ARP provisions.

In Britain most houses that had the garden or backyard space were provided with Anderson shelters, custom-made dugouts with a shell of strong cast-iron and bolstered with sandbags. They were supplied free to those whose houses had a low Poor Law Valuation (PLV), the figure used for the calculation of local goverment rates. Called after

Sir John Anderson (1882–1958) who was Home Secretary (1939–40), they were effective against the commonest cause of death in raids, falling masonry. It was reckoned that there were 4,000 dwellings with these private shelters, amounting to fewer than 15 percent of Belfast houses. For those too ill or frail to move far another type of shelter called the Morrison, after Herbert Morrison (1888–1965), Home Secretary (1940–45), was devised. It consisted of a large steel cage equipped with a spring base to take a mattress and set up in the biggest downstairs room of the house. The sluggish government took an unconscionable time to provide any of these necessities, as it seemed to Westminster. Eventually the money was made available. A feature of life at the time was remarkably high taxation, the most notorious money-raising device being the 'post-war credits', income tax levied at ten shillings in the pound credited to individuals for repayment after the war. They were paid to those who survived (and kept the certificates) in 1973. Various Northern Ireland officials argued that since their people were taxed as punitively as those in Britain that they should be entitled to the same level of financial aid.

By the summer of 1940 German forces controlled the coasts of Europe from the Arctic to the Pyrenees and in spite of all wishful thinking to the contrary Belfast was then well inside the range of the Luftwaffe bombers. With typical Teutonic efficiency their photographic arm had already got a clear picture of the city, its strategic targets and its dearth of defensive installations. As early as July 1940 reconnaissance Dorniers and Heinkels equipped with the latest Zeiss cameras had the target zone precisely marked out. On Friday, 18 October they obtained clear pictures of *das Flugzeugwerk* ('the aircraft factory', Short & Harland); *die Schiffswerft,* ('the shipyard', Harland & Wolff); *das Elektrisches Hauptkraftwerk Nordirlands* ('Northern Ireland's chief power station', Belfast Harbour); *die Grossmühle* ('the great mill', Rank's flour mill); *das Wasserwerk* ('the waterworks', Belfast Waterworks); *die Victoria Kaserne* (Victoria Barracks) and *Tankanlage am Conns Water* (Connswater Reservoir). They also pinpointed the gasworks, and those whose job it was to interpret their reconnaissance pictures realised that heavy-explosive bombs successfully delivered there would have a devastating radial effect on the centre of the city.

Apart from identifying targets the photographs made clear that anti-aircraft installations, known to the army as 'ack-ack', were sparse. ('Ack-ack' stood for AA in the old signallers' alphabet; nowadays it would be known as 'alpha-alpha', which does not have the same harsh urgency.) They noticed one heavy ack-ack gun at the Customs House near the Queen's Bridge and another battery on the Clarendon Dock at Donegall Quay. Another was in position in Victoria Park across the Island where the main shipyard was sited and there were two further emplacements on the east side of Belfast Lough at Holywood. The recommended ack-ack provision for the city was twenty-four Bofors 40mm cannons, and the same number of 3.7-inch guns. In fact there were only two Bofors and seven of the larger bore. Furthermore there were no searchlights, few barrage balloons, no means of creating a smokescreen and inadequate fighter protection. There was a squadron of Hurricanes based at Aldergrove but they were only fully effective in daylight. It should have been clear even to the blinkered Stormont government that because of the excellence of the German intelligence services that the *Wehrmacht* would have realised just how strategic a target Belfast actually was, with its aircraft factory, shipyard (that also made tanks), engineering plant, linen mills and rope works. Considering, too, the part the cigarette played in keeping up civilian and service morale, as is clear from contemporary films, they might well have regarded Gallahers' huge tobacco factory in York Street as another important target. In fact Gallahers were exemplary employers in that they provided effective air-raid shelters for their workforce.

As we have noted the aircraft factory had been in production for more than two years as a subsidiary of Short Brothers of Rochester in Kent. It was ideally suited to the manufacture of the large Sunderland flying boats because of the proximity of the sheltered lough, the already existing runways of the Belfast airport and a skilled workforce. Though by the start of the war the firm was employing up to twenty thousand workers, they soon established a reputation for low morale, poor production levels and frequency of strikes. The Germans would probably have been unaware of these internal difficulties; they were very aware that the plant was one of the main sources of the Stirling heavy bombers. In fact the company produced a total of 238 of these plus 133 Sunderlands. Harland & Wolff continued to build and repair ships, both as transports and those meant for war. They delivered 170 lighter warships, mainly cruisers, corvettes, destroyers and minesweepers, and two aircraft carriers, the *Formidable*, commissioned early in 1940, and the *Penelope*. They and the yards associated with them in Derry, Govan, and Liverpool repaired more than 30,000 vessels. The firm also made components for 550 tanks, which were finally assembled at Carrickfergus. The linen mills and rope works also played their part in what was known in a whole range of feeling from exaltation to utter cynicism as the 'war effort'. Two million parachutes, fabric for plane structures and building repairs, army uniforms and shirts – especially in Derry, the shirt capital of the western world – were produced by the mills and factories. A constant supply of rope was essential not only for the navy but also for the RAF and in fact the huge Belfast works supplied one third of the rope and cordage that the War Office required. They also made the survival buoyancy jackets, that were known as 'Mae Wests', after the pneumatic appearance of the popular, raunchy film star (1892–1980) of the period.

Belfast made and was continuing to make such an obvious contribution to the war effort that it was bound to become a target for the bombers. Some evidence of ARP did exist: protective trenches, dug in parks and schools and abandoned after Munich, were reopened in the first weeks of the war; gasmasks were distributed but few bothered to carry them, even after extra mustard-gas filters were added. Adult masks were usually of two standard sizes (for different sexes) with adjustable heavy rubber straps and Perspex panels for sight. They were hot and uncomfortable to wear and must have been dreadful for those suffering from any hint of claustrophobia. To give a positive gloss to the murky business of gas warfare they were known as respirators and, though delivered later to Belfast than to other cities, were distributed to the whole population. Children were fitted from a greater variety of sizes and during the fitting in mobile structures, as a kind of dread warning, were allowed to sample a whiff of the gas without the mask. In those less officious days the dire patron saint of the nanny state, Elfan Safetee, was relatively quiescent; security considerations were simpler. They were delivered to all houses, residential homes and orphanages and even to boarding schools, where they lay in piles unused until a few relics were resurrected to play a part against CS gas during the Battle of the Bogside in August 1969 in Derry. The briefly resurgent IRA held a rally in June 1939 at which a number of respirators were set on fire. It was not the most far-sighted action, whatever about its emotional appeal. Perhaps it is further proof of disbelief that the anti-British Germans would consider Belfast as a civilian target.

In fact gas attacks were regarded as unlikely. Their use, though horrific in their effects in the Great War, had been problematic, their effectiveness often nihilised by contrary winds. Air raids were a different matter. Baldwin's bombers would always get through but the accepted if blinkered wisdom still insisted that Belfast would not be involved. It proved hard to interest the citizenry in ARP. There were not many volunteers and when the existing air-raid wardens called to deliver the respirators the only insignia they could show was an armband; the blue uniforms and steel helmets had not arrived. The general lack of alarm was shared, as we have seen, by the city fathers, the Stormont parliament and even the cabinet, with a few exceptions. Some trenches were constructed on open ground but they were not only inadequate, lacking a properly protective cover, but as the clear-sighted Spender realised, they might actually be dangerous.

He had inspected the ones dug in front of the City Hall and felt that they would be deathtraps rather than shelters. With his usual directness he dismissed them as mere demonstration that the authorities were doing *something*.

MacDermott, whose appointment as Minister of Public Security in June 1940 was one of Craigavon's few wise decisions, immediately realised the inadequacy of the defensive provision that existed. He was amazed to discover that fire-fighting equipment had been returned to London as expensive and not really required in Belfast. (As ever central and local government's main preoccupation was even in wartime to keep the burden on the ratepayers as light as possible.) His task until the raids began had been thankless. The 'Phoney War', as it was called, seemed to confirm the wisdom of inaction. The period between the fall of Poland in September 1939 and the German invasion of Denmark and Norway in April 1940 had been relatively quiet in Europe at least. Only Germany, France and Britain were officially at war. The 'phoniness' may have been caused by internal struggles within the German High Command as to the next military move or it may have been intended to lull the Allies into a false sense of security. By July 1940 *la drôle de guerre*, as the French called it, was certainly over; France had fallen and 'fortress Europe' was in the hands of German forces, controlled along almost its whole costal length by the triumphant and highly efficient *Wehrmacht*.

MacDermott was the only member of the cabinet, with the possible exception of Sir Basil Brooke, the Minister of Agriculture, who had military experience from the Great War, and who seemed to understand how things had changed in the ten months of the war. He immediately ordered the evacuation and billeting in the country of 70,000 Belfast children, but only 7,000 appeared on the day and a similar call in August during the Battle of Britain for 5,000 evacuees registered as willing produced 1,800. Many from both drafts soon made their way home again, to the great relief of most of the reluctant people they were billeted on.

It became MacDermott's particular responsibility to make sure that there were sufficient shelters to protect the public in case of raids. The centre of Belfast on both sides of the estuary of the Lagan is built on sleech, a wet mobile peaty swamp that made the construction of deep tunnel-shelters impossible. The alternative of providing Anderson shelters for individual houses had made little progress. Fifty thousand homes were entitled to have them supplied but they were expensive and neither governmental nor municipal authorities would move until Westminster would let them know what financial aid they could expect from central government.

MacDermott's only real alternative was to build public shelters at surface level. They were constructed of redbrick (Belfast's favourite material) strengthened with steel rods. To say they were unsightly would be a considerable understatement; they were equalled in ugliness and probably pointlessness only by the equally gross water tanks that appeared in many localities after the 'Fire Raid' of May 1941, labelled EWS (emergency water supply). These linked static water tanks were constructed because of the complete failure of pumped water to quench the fires in the May raid. It took about a week before they became serious health hazards as well as having the risk of drowning. The shelters were literally empty shells; they may have been shrapnel- and incendiary-proof but a high explosive (HE) bomb falling anywhere near would have demolished the structure and any of the public who would have been so foolish as to take refuge there. None was fit to withstand the 1,100lb bombs that were dropped by the raiders. They could just about suffer a 500lb attack but that was the limit. In the summer of 1940 when it seemed that Britain stood alone and British cities were being bombed nightly, there were only 500 shelters in the whole of Northern Ireland, 200 of them in Belfast. At the beginning they had doors of wooden lath, locked when not in use. These soon disappeared during the bonfire season and the shelters became unofficial public toilets or refuges for illicit lovers. Though a hazard even to the limited traffic of the day they provided the children with extra opportunities for hide-and-seek, just as the EWS containers later allowed them to sail paper boats. They played a memorable part in *Odd Man Out* (1947), the brilliant film shot in Belfast by Carol Reed (1906–1976), but were in fact rarely used for their formal purpose.

The Luftwaffe had on the night of 14 November 1940 dropped 150,000 incendiary bombs, 130 parachute mines and 1,400 HEs on the city of Coventry in the Midlands of England. The Germans, in honour of the occasion, had invented a new verb, *koventrieren* ('obliterate'). The city had a population about half of that of Belfast and on that one night 568 people died, 4,330 houses were totally destroyed and ten times that number seriously damaged. Most of its factories, especially those making munitions, were reduced to rubble. Coventry's chief contribution to the war effort was the making of Rolls-Royce engines for planes but the raiders were unselective. The ack-ack barrage was grossly inadequate and the night fighters were unable to make much impact on the bombers. When the extent of the damage was made known MacDermott realised that Belfast could be treated in the same way. It was only 250 miles further than Coventry as the Dornier flies and if not as strategically important it was still worthy of attention. Coventry's gas and water mains, power lines, telephone communications and sewage pipes were all destroyed; roads and railways were blocked and when fire crews from all over the densely populated Midlands arrived to help they found that their connections did not fit the city's sources. The news terrified MacDermott because he knew how rapidly the same kind of disaster could overwhelm the much less prepared Belfast.

One result of this realisation of the utter chaos that would follow if (or when) the Germans should try *Koventrierung* in Belfast was the formulation of a plan that would place control in the hands of a few officials who would be granted special powers to get the city running again. MacDermott assigned the task to his deputy William Iliff, who had survived the evacuation at Dunkirk. As one well acquainted with the Old Testament, he wryly named it the Hiram Plan after the eleventh-century king of Tyre, who was an ally and friend of King David and supplied him with masons, carpenters, workmen and materials to build his gorgeous cedarwood palace in a Jerusalem at last at peace. Spender, the Belfast equivalent of Sir Humphrey in the television series *Yes, Minister*, was very much against devolving such power to MacDermott and his colleagues, believing like all top civil servants that running a country was too important a business to be left to politicians, however efficient. He realised that in the worst case the result would be chaos followed by the inevitably crude result of martial law. Belfast was lucky with essentially only three visitations, horrific though they were, but the Hiram Plan when put even briefly into action failed utterly when it tried to deal with the floods of refugees after the April raids.

By the spring of 1941 the war seemed to be going exactly as Hitler wanted it. The German armies had occupied Greece and Yugoslavia and would soon make the Napoleonic mistake of invading Russia. Craigavon was no longer capable of offering leadership and Andrews, born the same year, was more concerned with his government's reputation to take the imaginative steps necessary to protect the public. The cabinet minutes revealed that their main preoccupation was the protection of LS Merrifield's minatory statue of Edward Carson that dominates the long Prince of Wales Avenue that leads from the Upper Dundonald Road gates to the parliament buildings at Stormont. The citizens of Belfast had experienced the awareness campaign in the press, cinema and radio that the Ministry of Information (MOI) had manfully produced and advice pamphlets arrived regularly by post. They were advised what to do in an air raid, what preparations to make beforehand, how to tell the difference between the air-raid warning and that for the 'All Clear'. (Factory hooters were used, giving short peremptory cries for warning and a long drawn out wail as if an expelled sigh of relief for danger past.) They were advised to have buckets of water and sand handy for neutralising incendiary bombs and where supplied shown how to work stirrup-pumps and where to direct the jet. The pamphlets, with illustrations of competent, well-dressed, handsome middle-class mummies and daddies knowing exactly 'What to do about Gas', seemed unsuitable for the use of essentially undefended workers and their families.

> If the gas rattles sound hold your breath or you may breathe in gas. Put on your gas mask wherever you are. If indoors, close windows. If out-of-doors, turn up collar, put on gloves or keep hands in pockets. Take shelter in nearest building.

People were urged to 'practise with your gas mask regularly' and under a section headed 'Hints to Mothers', there was the not very convincing reassurance: 'Toddlers soon learn to put on their own masks. Let them make a game of it and they will soon wear their gas masks happily.'

Inept and written, it seemed, with no real experience of family life, especially in small backstreet dwellings, these pamphlets seem almost funny to our eyes nowadays. Yet what else could the authorities do but send out the booklets and hope for the best. The strangeness and only intermittent terror of life in wartime was compounded by the introduction of ration books and identity cards in 1940. It was a system that worked with little complaint because it was rigorously fair (except for those who could afford the usually available black-market goods). Britain imported much of its foodstuffs and all of its petrol but so successful was the Atlantic U-boat campaign in sinking merchant ships, especially in the early years of the war, that tea, butter, eggs, meat, sweets and biscuits were available only in short measure. Rationing continued until 1953 with bread 'put on the ration' for a period in 1946. Even in the early 1950s each adult was allowed two ounces of butter, four ounces of margarine and eight ounces of sugar per week. Clothes were also rationed with a points system that enabled people eventually to have saved enough to buy a suit but one with no turn-ups in the trousers, normal now but then an indication of dreadful austerity. There was also an active black market in clothing coupons. Many poor families who had little hope of affording new clothes could turn their coupons to financial advantage. Holidaymakers packed identity cards and ration books as a necessary part of their luggage.

There was no real reason why Belfast people should have to go short of dairy products, meat or eggs, since Northern Ireland, urged on by Brooke, increased agricultural production during the war. Most of their ration surplus, however, was shipped to Britain to feed the people there. It was seen as only fair that loyal Ulster should share the privations of their kin across the Irish Sea. Yet less than forty miles from Belfast and less than three miles from Derry was a land rich in butter, eggs, cheese and good red meat but notably lacking in tea. The ration for Éire citizens was one half-ounce of tea per week. A famous cartoon in the humorous *Dublin Opinion* showed a distracted housewife with a teapot in her hand being glared at by her large family; the caption read: 'The Wizard of $^1/_2$ Oz', a tribute to the most popular film of the time. The result was an increase in personal compensatory smuggling of 'dutiable goods' and a rich mythology of wonder tales of near misses and quick thinking in outwitting the excise men. One of the miseries of wartime food more exasperating than the total unavailability of bananas and oranges was the 'powdered egg'. It could in the hands of the very skilful make bearable scrambled eggs and with genius become an ingredient of cakes. Pamphlets on food advice became as prevalent as security literature and the Minister of Food, Lord Woolton (1883–1964), was held responsible – unfortunately not at a War Crimes tribunal – for the 'Woolton Pie', a meatless dish of carrots, parsnips, turnips and potatoes, covered with white sauce and pastry.

So, for the first year of the war Northern Ireland citizens got used to a kind of healthy austerity. Life was certainly more interesting than it had been in peacetime. Belfast was full of soldiers and Derry of sailors and all this talk of air raids seemed a kind of fantasy. There was a lot more money around since unemployment was at its lowest since the founding of the state. Cigarettes became scarce from time to time and razor blades had to be used beyond their proper life, with a few more shaves obtained when they were sharpened on the insides of glass tumblers. (Strange that no one except seafarers thought of growing beards.) Most of the picture houses were 'continuous from 2pm' and there was always a queue for the second house. You could always shut your eyes during the MOI bits and enjoy Hollywood magic – British films could not yet compete. Billboards were another medium for getting the message across. Everywhere you looked you were admonished to 'dig for victory' and 'save for victory'. You were challenged: 'Is your journey really necessary?' and told: 'Don't be a squander bug!' The most agreeable of these messages were the drawings of the brilliant artist 'Fougasse' (Cyril Kenneth Bird [1887–1965]), later editor of *Punch*, whose 'Careless Talk Costs Lives' posters showed drawings of Hitler on the luggage racks of train compartments, at the next table in wartime restaurants or lurking round corners listening to every word. (A fougasse was a not very reliable landmine used in the Great War in which Bird had been a Royal Engineer.) Life was much more than tolerable, the irritating insistence of some people that the city was going to be bombed dismissed as another minor irritation like the blackout.

The blackout (that was utterly meaningless on clear moonless nights, giving rise to the wartime lunar description 'a bomber's moon') required all buildings to have curtains of impermeable black material. (Windows were also X'd with the contemporary inferior forerunner of duct tape to strengthen them against blast damage.) There were no longer brightly lit shop windows against which Dickensian urchins might press their longing noses at Christmas time. Tram, bus and car headlights were masked with metal covers that let light through horizontal slits. Not that there was any petrol available to civilians except those in reserved occupations such as priests, doctors and other emergency personnel. Air-raid wardens had the task of checking that the blackouts were complete and it gave some temperaments the opportunity to rail at unfortunates whose masking was imperfect. Prosecutions for blackout infringements reached a total of 1,000 a month, well beyond the capability of even the most assiduous magistrates. Blackouts had not helped London much since the navigators could easily mark the Thames estuary and follow the river up to Tower Bridge. Belfast was even more of a sitter with the silver sheen of the lough marking where the shipyard and other strategic installations were sited. Even more ludicrous was the situation in border towns. Strabane was dark but Lifford, less than half a mile away across the River Mourne, looked like a luxury liner dressed all over, and in Pettigo, County Donegal, where the border runs through the main street, one half was black and the other bright. After the first Belfast air raid it was pointed out that the lighthouse on the Copelands had swept the Irish Sea with its welcoming beams all night long.

The cry, 'Don't you know there's a war on?', was used on many occasions to bully civilians and conceal inefficiency in officialdom. Pedestrians carried hand torches, called then flashlamps, but batteries and bulbs were like most other utter non-essentials hard to get. One County Down farmer attempting to buy a new whetstone to sharpen his scythe was told they were unobtainable because of the war. He wondered aloud with vituperative digressions were they throwing the (expletive-deleted) things at the Germans. Newspapers were scaled down to an absolute minimum and the paperback book came into its own. By the autumn of 1943, however, the blackout was upgraded to a 'dim-out' and the church bells that were to ring only as warning of a German invasion were heard again of a Sunday morning.

3

Blitzkrieg

THE GERMAN WORD BLITZKRIEG LITERALLY MEANT 'lightning war'. The most striking example of *Blitzkrieg* at work was the obliteration of most of the centre of the city of Rotterdam in Holland by Stuka dive-bombers on the morning of 10 May 1940 while paratroopers seized the airport and the bridges over the canals. (The phlegmatic Dutch city fathers found time that afternoon to call a meeting to plan the rebuilding of their city.) The same technique was begun for Britain in September 1940 and continued unmercifully until May 1941 with a brief lull during severe winter weather. The word *Blitzkrieg* was shortened by the British press to 'Blitz' and of the 127 large-scale raids seventy-one were targeted on London. Two million homes (60 percent of these in the capital) were destroyed by more than a hundred tons of bombs. There were more than 80,000 civilian casualties, half of the total for the whole war. Other cities attacked included Liverpool, Birmingham, Glasgow-Clydeside, Cardiff, Newcastle-Tyneside, Plymouth, Coventry (as we have noted) – and Belfast. In a way Belfast was unlucky. Its attacks came towards the end of the largely unsuccessful campaign that suggested that blanket bombing of civilian targets was strategically ineffective. War production continued almost unabated, helped by the stoicism of the people. Contemporary (and later) stories of British grit as an exemplification of the 'spirit of the Blitz' were rather exaggerated. Yet the amount of cowardice, self-seeking and panic was less than expected and the probability of some kind of popular revolution against the war remained low.

By 21 May 1941, 90 percent of Luftwaffe bombers had left for the Eastern Front, the spearhead of Operation Barbarossa that was intended to deliver to Hitler the mineral resources of Siberia and the Urals, and especially the oil deposits of the Ukraine. It was typical of Hitler's wishful megalomania that he should name it after Frederick I (1122–90), the German Holy Roman Emperor, famous for his red beard. If the decision to invade Russia had been made even a month earlier Belfast might have been spared its holocaust and those who scoffed at the possibility of air raids might have been vindicated. Barbarossa was Hitler's alternative to Operation Sealion, the invasion of England. When Fighter Command of the RAF effectively defeated the Luftwaffe in the Battle of Britain (July–October 1940) with Hurricanes and the Spitfires that had arrived just in time, Hitler decided to postpone Sealion. He had always a strange reluctance to crush Britain, hoping perhaps to make her an ally against the USSR and its communist leader Josef Stalin. In his rather skewed logic Barbarossa was part of the same crusade as Sealion.

Attacking Belfast was as logical and as strategically sound as bombing any of the English cities. The German equivalent of the Bomber Command had amassed a file of intelligence documents, boosted by excellent photographs of the city. These had been garnered by swift and elusive reconnaissance flights. One of the earliest, probably the third such foray, took place on Saturday, 30 November 1940, two days after Craigavon's funeral to Stormont. It confirmed intelligence already garnered and confirmed also the identifiable aspects of the east coast with the elongated U-shaped Belfast Lough and the long finger of the Ards peninsula almost locking in the bright Strangford Lough. Unless visibility was very bad those two marine loughs would highlight the way to the city and the bombers' targets.

One of the more cogent reasons for discounting the likelihood of air raids was that the planes' flight-path would have them fly over 'more attractive' targets than Belfast's. It was also argued that the distance of 'over 1,000 miles' would have passed the edge of tolerance for heavily loaded bombers. German intelligence findings, however, had made it clear that not only Belfast's munitions works but also her general industries were appropriate and sufficiently attractive targets. Further, the distance from occupied Brittany to Belfast was rather less than 500 miles and the direct route was mainly over the Celtic and Irish Seas where there were no ack-ack batteries.

By March 1941 the Luftwaffe was primed to bomb the city. Another motive for raids was that Belfast was Ireland's chief port and therefore a logical part of the current campaign against maritime towns. Indeed, it was nearly as worthy a target as Liverpool or Plymouth. Derry, as the most westerly Allied European port, had assumed a significant role in the Battle of the Atlantic and had also to be considered an appropriate target. It became the chief base for Atlantic shipping, both merchant and naval, at one stage harbouring 140 Allied ships. It was also one of the chief repair sites for ships damaged in battle. A new graving dock had been built for the purpose and close to the river was a submarine training school built by American civilian technicians. The second city was lucky in that, in the only raid, on the night of Easter Tuesday, 15–16 April 1941, only two parachute mines were dropped. Belfast was a more substantial target and it received its greatest battering on that night. By then it had already had some experience of bombing. MacDermott, though as firmly anti-nationalist as his older Unionist colleagues, was younger (in his mid-forties) and much more talented. He had studied carefully the reports about the nature and the extent of the devastation of Coventry, Birmingham and Plymouth, and was fully aware of how vulnerable Belfast was. As he observed in his plea to the War Office on 21 March for more heavy ack-ack, barrage balloons and night fighters:

> Up to now we have escaped attack. So had Clydeside until recently.
> Clydeside got its blitz during the period of the last moon. There [is] ground
> for thinking that… the enemy could not easily reach Belfast in force except
> during a period of moonlight. The period of the next moon from say the
> 7th to the 16th April may well bring our turn.

A copy of his memo was sent out of courtesy to Andrews but without much expectation of response.

MacDermott's forecast was precisely right. On 8 April, the Tuesday of Holy Week, at 00.04 hours, six Heinkel HE 111 bombers, some from the crack pathfinder echelon *Kampfgruppe* 26 based in northern France, arrived on a kind of exploratory mission to test the city's defences. They had been part of a group later joined by others based in Soesterberg in Holland, on the periphery of a much larger strike force sent to attack, among other targets, Glasgow. These planes, fifteen in all, were assigned the target of Dumbarton, then an important shipbuilding town on the north bank of the Clyde with a population of about 25,000 people. If the weather were to prove unsuitable then they were to attack Liverpool or, failing that, Newcastle-on-Tyne. The seventh to eighth of April was one of the single greatest nights ever of widespread bombing by the Luftwaffe involving a total of 517 planes, directed against the usual targets: London, Glasgow, Liverpool and Bristol. The Dumbarton contingent went west along the English Channel, rounded Lizard Point in Cornwall and, flying over Irish air space, crossed into Scotland at Wigton and reached the target only to find it covered with dense cloud. (German meteorological predictions were usually accurate.)

The six Belfast Heinkels may have been sent on a fishing expedition, probably ordered to cross the North Channel as being superfluous to requirements in Glasgow or Liverpool. One can imagine Luftwaffenmajor Schwarz (played in the movie by Anton Diffring) telling Fritz, Hans, Horst and the rest to pop across and have a look. The five barrage balloons were too low to hinder their run-in at 7,000 feet. The principle of these huge blimps was that they were sent to a height greater than the path of the bombers and so formed a barrier with their steel cables that would interrupt the direct line of flight of the attacking planes. That night they were deployed too low and the Heinkels flew above them, so confident of safety that they kept on their navigation lights and dropped flares on the Island. As they made their sortie, so contemptuous were they of Belfast's ack-ack deployment that they displayed barely minimum caution, at times risking a path lower than the maximum covered by the barrage balloon steel cables, dropping their fizzing fire bombs with full lights on show.

HE bombs demolished a grain store that was part of the *Grossmühle*, the Rank flour mill that had already been selected by the reconnaissance planes in their earlier exploratory flights in July 1940. Sewers were damaged and though some bombs fell on the docks where merchant vessels were berthed they, armed with ack-ack guns since the beginning of the war, did not attempt to engage because they had no system of telephone contact with the batteries on shore. This typical lack of communication was to have a deleterious effect eight days later when the Luftwaffe returned in force. Though only incidentally an air raid the night's sortie could claim one excellent result. As well as incendiary and HE bombs the Germans used another type of aerial weapon, the land mine. These could not be aimed with the precision of the others but floated down gently on parachutes. One landed on the roof of Shorts aircraft factory with the kind of chance, lucky or unfortunate, that seems a recurring if inexplicable part of warfare. Contemporary newspaper and official photographs show widespread devastation: roofless workshops, lumps of shattered masonry, scattered pieces of fuselage and steel girders twisted into fantastic shapes. The workers on the night shift thought that the raid was over when at 3.30, after a last sweep by a bomber, they saw the parachute mine being blown by the wind right on to the roof of the fuselage shop. Four and a half acres of factory workshops were completely destroyed, as were the components of fifty fuselages intended for the Stirling bombers that were Shorts' main contribution to the war effort.

The death toll of fifteen, including two members of the Auxiliary Fire Service (AFS) and one accidental death at Balmoral, when a soldier was killed after an ack-ack gun misfired, was small by any standards and certainly minuscule in comparison with that experienced in the other cities attacked that night. In fact one of the Belfast raiders was shot down by a Hurricane scrambled in spite of the cloudy night. The fighter was one of Squadron No. 245 based at RAF Aldergrove and piloted by Squadron-Leader JWC Simpson DFC. He tracked two of the Heinkels to the County Down coast off the Lecale peninsula and blew one to pieces. The report in the *Belfast Telegraph* that evening, reflecting the heavy censorship and obsessional fear of 'careless talk', simply said under a sub-headline 'North's First Blitz: Night of Thrills':

> Ground defences were in action and one of the raiders was brought down by a night fighter.

A German report written about the raid after debriefing noted that two huge fires had been started *auf Kaianlage* ('on the docks') and that unlike the other targets for that night – Greenock, Birmingham, Liverpool, Bristol, Glasgow, Great Yarmouth, Harwich, Plymouth, Swansea, Barrow, Hull, and St Austell (in Cornwall) – where the flak (anti-aircraft response) had been 'middle to heavy', in Belfast it was written of as *geringe* ('slight'). A more detailed German debriefing later described the defences as 'inferior in quality, scanty and insufficient'.

The total strength of ack-ack batteries in Northern Ireland as a whole in fact consisted of twenty-four heavy and fourteen light guns. Most of these were used for the defence of Belfast, the heavy guns peripherally located on hills around the city, the latter concentrated in the harbour area. There were six radar stations, no formally organised system of observers and only one bomb-disposal unit. No wonder the flak level was considered '*geringe*'. MacDermott's report sent as a matter of form to the cabinet office was brief, if a little bit optimistic:

> A small force of enemy bombers dropped a number of incendiary bombs on Belfast between 0010 and 0330. One major fire was started at the timber yards in Duncrue Street and about twelve small fires in the Newtownards Road area. The latter were got under control quickly, but St Patrick's Church was damaged. Fires were started later at Alexandra Works and Victoria Shipyards in Harland & Wolff. All were got under control by daylight.

This report that was rushed to London early on the morning of Tuesday, 8 April, in its terse but cheery way, made no reference to the landmine that had wreaked such damage in Shorts. Less dramatic but very damaging to the reputation of the civil defence workers was the 'small fire' at McCue Dick's timber yard in Duncrue Street. The fire service were overstretched and could not arrive until ninety minutes after the initial impact of the parachute mine that started the conflagration. The burning yard, fuelled by highly flammable wood and tar, its flames reflected in the lough, lit up the whole west harbour area better than any enemy flare. By the time the fire-fighters arrived the water mains had been fractured by the HE bombs, drastically reducing the water pressure.

The events of that April night scattered any illusions about Belfast as an unlikely target. It may have been a trivial, even peripheral, raid from the Luftwaffe's viewpoint but it caused a turmoil of mixed emotions among Belfast people. The most prominent was a sense of fear and dismay. The unbelievable had happened and a majority did not quite know how to deal with the unease. The night did more than all the pamphlets, broadcasts and films to show what a bombing raid actually meant. There were, of course, cases of individual bravery: some of the housewives in the Newtownards Road dealt with the incendiaries by wrapping them in blankets and removing them to places of safety. One in a rage picked up a bomb with a pair of tongs and threw it out into the middle of the street. The welfare services were seen to be less than adequate. Two hundred people from the neighbourhood of Alexandra Park Avenue were moved to a local hall because of an unexploded bomb and kept there while it was eventually defused. There was no food for them. As a result volunteering by housewives in the Women's Voluntary Service (WVS) increased dramatically. The AFS and the Civil Defence units also found many more volunteers and there was a good response to calls for blood donors. Attempts were quickly made to bolster the transparently inadequate air-raid precautions. Some searchlight equipment arrived by ship to Larne on Thursday, 10 April and another light anti-aircraft battery dispatched that day arrived on Friday evening. These long-overdue actions may have eased the consciences of the authorities but before they could be made effective it was already too late.

The most significant result of the raid was the realisation by the people that the Luftwaffe would certainly return. The question of evacuation became a priority as did the relocation of those whose homes had been destroyed. Yet here too events, those imponderable entities, prevented any adequate implementation of even the minimal options at the disposal of the Northern Ireland authorities. Organised evacuation proved impossible and the numbers requiring alternative accommodation soared. Arrangements for another wave of evacuation was planned for 16 April and clothes and food were stockpiled in the many welfare centres. There were many alerts in the days that followed, at least once every twenty-four hours, but they were treated as practices. There had been regular use of sirens each time an enemy plane was caught on the radar over the Irish Sea so little attention was paid. Churchgoers leaving the Holy Family church at Newington after the Mass of the Pre-Sanctified on Good Friday morning were 'buzzed' by a plane that they were convinced was German. There was a distinctive sound to the engines of Luftwaffe planes, sufficiently different to those of the RAF, to make them identifiable as hostile. The noise they made was not continuous but broken as if the planes had intermittent cardiac trouble and were in sore need of defibrillation. Belfast people got into the habit of listening carefully to any aerial engine noise and reacting accordingly.

It was, however, Eastertide and the citizens of Belfast continued instinctively to behave as if there were no danger. The Irish Tourist Board (ITB) had an office in 28 Howard Street and though they could hardly promise sun-drenched beaches they had plenty to offer in the realm of unrationed meat, butter, eggs and bacon, and liquor. There is an Irish phrase, *togha gach bia agus rogha gach dí* ('the best of all kinds of food and drink') and Éire hotels liked to suggest that they still could provide it. Tea was admittedly a bit scarce, sugar rather coarse and the bread had 'nowt taken out' but they could still supply the *real* necessities of life in contrast to Spartan Belfast. An ITB advertisement that appeared in the *Belfast News Letter* on Wednesday, 9 April, the day after the raid, headed 'Easter Holidays', made no mention of rations but reminded readers:

> Easter approaches and that extra hour of sunshine and light this year provides a rare opportunity for out-of-doors enjoyment. For your health's sake rest, relax or recreate in fresh surroundings – enjoy the exhilarating tonic of the Irish spring.

Apart from the dodgy use of 'recreate' as an intransitive verb it was an attractive item, even if a little bit optimistic about the Irish spring. The illustration showed a pair of young adults climbing on the top of an Irish mountain. Both had small rucksacks, the man in shorts and the colleen in a decent knee-length tweed skirt. She carried an alpenstock presumably for self-protection and they both had an air of well-bred health. Under the drawing was a set of golf clubs draped across a suitcase. Potential tourists were reminded that, 'The Transport Companies have arranged special services at reduced fares.' The advertisement concluded with the admonition: 'Make your plans now.' It was and is a guaranteed way of making God laugh. Nationalists especially in the west of the province travelled regularly to Dublin on such a jaunt – that is when they didn't pop over the border to Donegal where the hotels had boom times – and Dublin had many British service personnel staying, in mufti, of course. The many members of the security forces had learned that trick as well. Holidays for younger people in Éire had received a boost with the foundation ten years earlier of the youth hostel movement, *An Óige*. Most hostels were within cycling distance of each other and Easter was a popular time for cyclists on roads empty apart from top-heavy, lumbering peat lorries.

For those who could not afford a holiday in the 'south of Ireland' (the site that newspaper reports of weddings nearly always gave as the destination for newly married Ulster couples on honeymoon) or those who were disinclined for political reasons to go *there*, there was always Bangor. In spite of barbed wire entanglements on the beaches of Helen's Bay and Ballyholme (a relic of the fears of invasion) it was the destination of many trippers intent on enjoying Easter Monday in the traditional way. The trains during the first mile of the journey had that day to pass the ruins of the wrecked fuselage factory but the passengers were not inclined to brood. The sirens may have sounded every day but they were generally ignored. In fact, on the night of the bank holiday, a single Luftwaffe plane flew over the city at the unreachable height of 22,000 feet.

Those who did not want to take advantage of the County Down Railway's offer of 'Bangor and Back for a Bob' went to a crowded Windsor Park to see a friendly between representative teams of the IFA and the FAI and were pleased that the visitors were beaten 2–1. There were some better than average pictures to be seen in Belfast's many cinemas – more than forty altogether. Showing in the new luxury Ritz was *Torrid Zone* (1940) with the popular Irish-American duo James Cagney (1899–1986) and Pat O'Brien (1899–1983), and in the older Royal, once a legitimate theatre, *It's in the Air* (1940), a typically funny comic movie with the popular George Formby (1904–1961) in which misadventures in the RAF were punctuated by the cheeky songs, accompanied on his banjolele, for which he was most famous. There was, indeed, plenty of Easter entertainment and there was no reason not to enjoy the holiday.

Easter Monday was perhaps the most popular of all dates for weddings, the first weekday after the end of Lent, the season of Church prohibition of 'nuptial feasts'. One couple, Bob and Nellie Bell, emerging from the Sinclair Seaman's Presbyterian Church in Corporation Street after their wedding ceremony at 1.30 pm, were struck by the paucity of bystanders; weddings usually attracted a crowd of well-wishers or the professionally curious. They had not realised that while they were signing the register the air-raid warning had sounded. The long drawn-out wail of the All Clear was not heard until the wedding meal in the Carlton Restaurant was about to begin. The bride was conscious that guests from the country were decidedly uneasy about staying late in the target city but most of the party had departed by that evening. In the quiet April evening the city, from Cave Hill to the Minnowburn Beeches, looked normally peaceful. It was difficult to believe that anything could disturb that peace, that normality.

Yet six days earlier people had died and many houses and businesses had been destroyed. As long as you looked south and kept your eyes averted from York Road, Garmoyle Street, the Pollock Dock, the Island, Shorts and many little streets on both sides of the Newtownards and Albertbridge Roads – Mourne, Hornby, Bright, Montrose, Belvoir, Kathleen, Glenallen, Kathleen, Heatley and many more that had been destroyed – all seemed serene. Many of these little streets have now gone, affected by the later troubles and slum clearance. They may have seemed to the outsider to represent minimal housing but that peripheral raid was the first blow against a focussed and caring local community with its own systems for survival and mutual aid. Even averting the eyes could not obliterate the memory of the noise of planes, ack-ack, and the gaudy pyrotechnics of the incendiaries. Many were distressed by the sight of the tower of St Patrick's Church, Ballymacarret blazing like a giant torch, while St Matthew's Catholic church in the Short Strand area escaped serious damage. In the more deadly raids that were to follow targets were examined with quiveringly sectarian antennae sensing religious conspiracy even here.

Paddy Carolan, a lad who wouldn't be ten years old until the following June, was an eyewitness or at least an earwitness to that first raid. The sirens went at four minutes past midnight when he was fast asleep in his home in 39 Marsden Gardens, off Cavehill Road. He was roused by an older sister, told to put on some clothes and join the family downstairs. One sister, Bridie, was crouching under a stout table and would not allow anyone to share her refuge. The rest – Paddy, his brother, three sisters, and their mother – made themselves as comfortable as they could under the stairs, in the lumber depository that they and many others called the 'glory hole'. It was, after all, the safest place in the house. Their father, DS Teddy Carolan, was on fire-watching duty at his local nick, Townhall Street police station, between Oxford Street and Victoria Street.

The night was passed with endless recitations of the Rosary that grew louder to match the intensity of the combined noises of bombs and ack-ack fire. They were not aware of any damage in the vicinity of Cavehill Road that night and the raid was over by dawn. In fact, a large parachute landmine devastated Sunningdale Park that ran from the other side of the Cavehill Road by Cliftonville golf course. Paddy remembers going out the back of their house after the All Clear with his eldest sister Nancie and seeing a huge fire down near the docks, almost certainly the conflagration at McCue Dick's timber yard.

An older sister, Marie, was a student at St Mary's Teacher Training College on the Falls Road. Among her personal possessions was a beeswax candle that had been blessed on Candlemas Day, two months previously. St Mary's was a boarding college and the Dominican sisters roused up the students from the dormitories and brought them to an assembly room downstairs. Marie was surprised when she was not allowed to light her holy candle but in this case the nuns preferred safety to devotion.

The people of the city were deeply shocked but the instinctive thirst for normality caused many sight-seekers to brave the series of craters, piles of rubble and diminished public transport to see the damage for themselves. On the afternoon of Easter Tuesday, Paddy, with his mother, brother and sister Bridie, went on such an exploratory walk. They entered Willowbank Gardens and crossed the Antrim Road to walk down Alexandra Park Avenue that led to York Road. At the foot they passed Grove School, where an unexploded bomb had caused the first-aid post located there to be moved temporarily south to Mountcollyer School on the Limestone Road. As they turned left into York Road they immediately began to see something of the devastation still lingering a week after the raid. They could see the remains of McCue Dick's timber yard in Duncrue Street, the burnt-out shell of the *Grossmühle,* the destruction of Northern Road to their right and the many small houses reduced to rubble along the Shore Road, and the even greater devastation on the Whitewell Road. When they reached Glengormley they were quite exhausted and glad to take a tram home to the stop at the Capitol Cinema nearest their Marsden Gardens home. The children had the longest walk of their young lives and were quite happy to go early to bed.

4

Easter Tuesday

EASTER MONDAY DREW TO ITS CLOSE and the trippers to Whitehead, Bangor and Donaghadee returned refreshed, many of them ready to start another week's work. They were relaxed, if a bit tired, and looking forward to a good night's sleep. It was interrupted by an alert as a single reconnaissance plane flew at 22,000 feet just in range of the one battery, HAA 102, at Lisnabreenagh, in County Down, to the southeast of the city, that fired ineffectual shells at it. The All Clear sounded quite soon and most people settled down to sleep again.

The morning after, Easter Tuesday, 15 April, was still a school holiday but many adults went to work on a dull, overcast day with Irish mist – that euphemism for Ulster's prevalent condition of drizzling rain. 'Lord Haw-Haw', the nickname bestowed by the journalist Jonah Barrington of the *Daily Express* on William Joyce (1906–46), had mentioned the city in one of his nightly propaganda broadcasts from Hamburg. He was born in America, brought up in County Mayo and Galway, and in 1934 was made head of research in Sir Oswald Mosley's (1896–1980) British Union of Fascists. He later founded his own party, the Nationalist Socialist League, and in 1939 travelled to Germany on a British passport. This was taken as sufficient proof of his guilt in his post-war trial for treason when he was sentenced to be hanged. His remarkable English accent that earned him the soubriquet seemed to be upper-class but had always an ersatz air about it when his nightly broadcasts began with the words, 'Germany calling; Germany calling.' His seasonal message that April began, 'There will be Easter eggs for Belfast.' As usual his propaganda was either ignored or derided but the spectators at a match in Windsor Park that afternoon could not help but notice a Junkers 107 circling overhead. There was no military response and the away team, Distillery, defeated their near neighbours Linfield 3–1. The Blues were not having a good Easter.

In Derry it was the second day of Féis Doire Colmcille, the weeklong Easter festival of Irish language, music and dance. The Tuesday evening was one of the highlights of the week since it was then that the Junior Action Song competition was held – a source of much rivalry between the city schools. The rain cleared from the west by early afternoon and the excited children and tenser parents queued to find seats in the Guildhall on a dry mild evening with scattered cloud and a light wind. When the sirens sounded shortly after half-past ten in the evening most of the children had gone home. The wardens went quickly to their posts and at the local ARP headquarters, also in the Guildhall, they listened with no great trepidation to see if it was just another lone plane spotted over the Irish Sea. Charles Gallagher, whose book *Acorns and Oak Leaves* (1981) gives a composite picture of his native city, recalled:

> The usual rumours – or buzzes – went the rounds. Then the shrill insistent ringing of the telephone, and everybody jumped. The operator answered and had a monosyllabic conversation with the person at the other end in ARP headquarters.
>
> 'Belfast is being hammered again,' she said laconically, as she replaced the receiver.

Belfast *was* being hammered; the sirens sounded at 22.40 and up to 200 German bombers, comprising Junkers Ju 88s, Heinkels HEIII, and Dorniers, attached to *Kampfgeschwäder* ('battle squadrons') 54 and 55 that had taken off from airfields at Evreux and Dreux, northwest of Paris, approached the city. They flew at a low level up the middle of the Irish Sea to avoid the radar stations on the Welsh coast and at Kilkeel. They passed over Éire air space at Dundalk, sped over Carlingford Lough and headed for Belfast via Dromore. The cloud had been dispersed by the breeze and though the moon was only three-quarters full, it lit up the no longer sleeping countryside. The unmistakable broken sound of the aircraft engines were heard by the townspeople as they flew past on their way to the targets: the docks, the shipyard and the plane factory. The first wave dropped their flares to light up the targets but seem to have mistaken the dull sheen of the Waterworks on the Antrim Road, lit by the pale moon, for the Herdman, Victoria and Musgrave Channels. The bombers came in continuous waves flying again at 7,000 feet to avoid the inadequate balloon barrage. Their bombs fell mainly on a sickle-shaped swathe that stretched from York Road at the LMS/NCC terminus in both directions saturating the lower Antrim Road and the foot of the Shankill. The HE bombs made the little Victorian slum houses fall like rows of dominos. A bomb landing on a single house was enough, in many cases, to cause the whole street to collapse. There was later much speculation about the attack on the Waterworks; recent research has made a case for them being a primary target so that in dealing with 'the many fires' the service would have had nothing to extinguish them because of low water pressure. The German intelligence sources may not have known that among many ships in the docks for refit and repair was the *Ark Royal*, one of the Royal Navy's largest aircraft carriers. She was sunk in the Mediterranean by a single torpedo the following November while returning from Malta to Gibraltar.

The intensity of the Belfast raid, whether misdirected or not, must have made it seem to the beleaguered inhabitants that the city was the premier target of the Luftwaffe that night, but other places shared the unwelcome attentions of the bombers. It was a good night, as we have seen, for the purpose. If not quite a 'bombers' moon' it did lend a ghostly light and in a sense the flares were not needed. There were diversionary raids on Barrow, Tyneside and Hull, mainly to keep RAF fighters busy but the main targets were Merseyside and Belfast, the designated forces separating over Cardigan Bay, off Central Wales. Liverpool, Birkenhead and the other Mersey towns were used to air raids and had already fairly reasonable systems for civilian protection. Belfast was virtually defenceless; the half on-street/half on-carriageway shelters were too few and were airless, smelly horrors. They also proved to be deathtraps. Late-night tram passengers, many on their way home from a dance in the Floral Hall, the city's most beautifully sited venue at the foot of Cavehill, famous for its romantic views of the lough, were stopped at the junction of the Antrim Road and Atlantic Avenue at Alexandra Park and ushered into one of the 'shelters'. They were crowded into the noisome stifling darkness and perished when a bomb penetrated the roof and the walls fell in on top of them. Most people preferred, in many cases wisely, to hide under the stairs in their own homes. The trouble with that decision was that even that most protected part of the house was vulnerable in a majority of the houses attacked. Brightness fell from the sky as 300 parachute flares lit up the areas that were afterwards to take the heaviest bombardment and these were followed by eighty parachute mines. People later remembered that the flares produced a light brighter than a summer noonday.

The southernmost point on the boundary of devastation was the intersection of Loopland Park and the Castlereagh Road. Moving north this demarcation line crossed the Sydenham Road at the Oval, Glentoran FC's ground, then ran in an almost semicircular arc to the Clarendon Dock, then north again by Mountcollyer Avenue to the Cavehill Road at the Waterworks. The south boundary, really a line running almost exactly northwest, stretched from the Loop River to Flax Street off the Crumlin Road. Another area that received the attention of the Luftwaffe was a patch that included Broadway and

Beechmount on the Falls Road. With the unemotional eye of history it is clear that the main casualties were civilians, a majority of whom lived in the slums that still clustered near the mills and in Sailortown where the shipyard workers lived. Twenty-nine thousand incendiaries fell on these working-class districts out of a total of 96,000 carried in 800 canisters. The heat generated by these firebombs was enough to melt steel. Six hundred and seventy-four HEs fell at a mean rate of 120 an hour. Many were fitted with steel nose-caps to prevent deeper penetration when the damage they were meant to cause would be limited. They did much more harm when kept to the surface, spreading the blast effect much wider.

Blast could have some bizarre effects. In his memoir *Climbing Slemish* (2007), the journalist Dennis Kennedy, who was five years old at the time and living in the comparative safety of Lisburn, tells how his father, a member then of the AFS, entered a bomb-damaged house off York Street and found it empty. Just to make sure he looked in the cupboard under the stairs and 'There, sitting tightly crowded together, was the entire family of five – the parents and three children. There was not a mark on them, but they were all dead.'

Another witness to the worst night of the Blitz was Anthony Powell (1905–2000), the author of the brilliant twelve-part novel sequence, *A Dance to the Music of Time* (1951–75). He served with the Welch Regiment and was stationed in Belfast during the early years of the war, though he was too detached in his stiff-lipped British way to name the place. In the eighth volume of the sequence, *The Soldier's Art* (1966), his alter ego Nick Jenkins describes the way, in the 'first local blitz – when they killed a thousand people', the flares descended:

> Clustered together in twos and threes, they drifted at first aimlessly in the breeze, after a time scarcely losing height, only swaying a little this way and that, metamorphosed into all but stationary lamps, apparently suspended by immensely elongated wires attached to an invisible ceiling.

As with the German 'Moaning Minnies' (*Minenwerfer*) of the Great War that made an eerie whistling sound on their trajectories, the HE bombs had small organ pipes fitted to their tailfins so that the screams from them as they fell would add to the terror. Also terrifying was the noise of the ack-ack batteries as they tried to shoot down the bombers. A sergeant who was in charge of an ack-ack emplacement at Lisnabreenagh told me later that he felt that guns generated nearly as much lethal shrapnel from the shells as did the bombers. This noise ceased at 1.45am because the main phone exchange at the corner of Oxford Street and East Bridge Street had been hit, depriving the place of all but the most primitive means of communication. The ack-ack batteries had no alternative but to cease to attempt to shoot down the bombers, not that they had been very successful anyway, though, according to German reports they did account for one bomber. Because of the almost complete breakdown of communication the Hurricanes at Aldergrove were unable to scramble due to fears that they should be vulnerable to friendly ack-ack fire, and had an exclusion area of five kilometres in radius centred in Belfast imposed upon them. When the raid was over, a Hurricane, piloted again by Simpson DFC, followed the flight-path and shot down a Junkers 88 over Ardglass.

One other trained literary eye was on the edge of the destruction: Sam Hanna Bell (1909–90), the novelist and radio features writer-producer, was an air-raid warden and eventually the man in charge of welfare in the city. He recalled the night of the 'heavy air attack' in a special number of the *Honest Ulsterman* (January 1980) entitled 'The War Years in Ulster 1939–45'.

> After the sharpish attack of April 8th many air raid wardens had left for the countryside. But many stayed. 'Catholic' and 'Protestant' sectors hastened to each other's assistance. It was a remarkable time. The sector in which I then lived, bounded approximately by Botanic Avenue and the Lagan had few incidents to report. We chain-smoked as we scurried around the streets, hiding the glowing butts from the Heinkels droning over the burning city. There was a scatter of incendiaries in McClure Street [running from Botanic Avenue to Ormeau Road] which we helped the NFS to smother. A landmine went off about Ormeau Park damaging

houses across the river. We wrestled with street doors blown halfway down hallways. From under the stairs of a house we extricated an old woman still clutching a miniature Union Jack. Some thought that the tree-lined avenues and streets misled the Luftwaffe into thinking that here the countryside began. Others held that we were saved by our proximity to the Malone Road.

As MacDermott had dreaded, the water mains and sewage pipes were fractured in the first wave and most of the telephone wires were cut. Individual members of the regular Fire Service and the AFS worked tirelessly through the six hours of the raid but there was not a great deal that they could do without water. Both services were totally unprepared for the intensity and the horror of a modern air attack. There has persisted a story that John Smith, the chief of the city fire service, gave up completely and spent the night weeping helplessly under his desk in Chichester Street Fire Station. He was an elderly Scot who had already been criticised for his refusal to liaise with the AFS and to see to their professional training. He was persuaded to resign on the grounds of ill-health on Thursday, 17 April.

That night's work all but crippled the city. With 100,000 people made homeless and basic amenities 'down', to use the current meiotic expression, there was some fear that the city might cease to work. Belfast had proved more vulnerable than even MacDermott had warned. The fatalities were mainly the innocent, many of them poverty-stricken, whose lives had no possible target value, unless the intention of the raid was to weaken the morale of the proletariat. Their morale was not all that high to begin with and for some, as the state of their evacuee children was to show, so primitive that they needed immediate welfare aid. If the Belfast blitz did no other good its revelation of the conditions that the poor had to undergo made it less than an entirely horrific event.

As a tactical raid it was not much of a success; the shipyards and docks were relatively undamaged. Only two planes in Shorts aircraft factory were destroyed. The boiler shop, the copper shop, the brass foundry and the bolt screwing shop in Harland & Wolff were all hit, delaying repair and building work. Four linen mills, Ewart's, Brookfield, Edenderry and York Street, were badly damaged, the collapse of the latter causing many collateral deaths as its high walls fell on the little mill houses in Sussex and Vere Streets. The LMS/NCC railway station on York Road was hit and the lines ruptured but they were repaired in time to deal with the surge of refugees. A margarine factory in Hudson Street (now gone, but near the ill-fated Percy Street), a mineral water factory in Bath Place (also gone), and the large Wilton Funeral Home on the Crumlin Road were razed to the ground. A sad corollary was the death of forty-seven magnificent black Belgian horses that had given a great air of solemnity to Belfast funerals. The professional skills of the staff and the mortuary of the last utility were grievously missed the next morning when the many dead had to be accommodated. It was reported that thirty businesses, seven motor works, seven stores, two schools, two cinemas, two tram depots, two hospitals and a nurses home in Frederick Street (the site of the old Royal Hospital) suffered greater or lesser damage.

The familiar buildings of the city centre do not seem to have been deliberately selected by the bombers, as later 'Baedecker' raids did. (These Luftwaffe raids begun in 1942 were deliberately planned to attack British cities with important cultural and historical buildings, such as Canterbury, Norwich and Bath, in revenge for Allied raids on Cologne and Lübeck. Karl Baedecker [1801–59] was the author of the standard nineteenth-century travellers' guides to all the cities of Europe.) Robinson Cleaver, the magnificent department store at the corner of Donegall Place and Donegall Square North, was quite unscathed. The overstated City Hall had serious roof damage but its twin sister, the Belfast College of Technology, escaped. This typically Victorian building had always been the despair of local aesthetes because its position spoiled the view of the elegant façade of Royal Belfast Academical Institute (known to all the city as Inst) that had been designed by the famous Georgian architect, Sir John Soane

(1753–1837). Inst, too, survived along with another of Belfast's admittedly few architectural treasures, Clifton House, once the Belfast Charitable Institute. Other notable survivors were the Queen's University of Belfast, designed by the ubiquitous Sir Charles Lanyon (1813–89), the Museum and Art Gallery at Stranmillis, and, remarkably, St George's Church (Belfast's first Anglican church), at the east end of High Street.

I say remarkably because that end of Royal Avenue and the streets immediately off it were badly damaged. High Street, North Street and Donegall Street were saturated with incendiaries and HEs. The west side of Royal Avenue did better than the east though it received its complement of blast and shrapnel damage. The Central Library bore the pock marks of the collateral damage for many years, as did the offices and works of the *Belfast Telegraph*. They managed to keep going and were able to help produce the city's morning papers when their offices and works were hit. The *Northern Whig*'s offices in Bridge Street were gutted in the 'Fire Raid' of 5 May but it continued to print, thanks to the fraternal help of the 'Telly'. The same facilities were also made available to the *Irish News* and the *Belfast News Letter*.

5

Death and Destruction

THE WAVES OF DESTRUCTION CONTINUED UNTIL 5am on the Wednesday morning. Figures of fatalities vary but it is agreed that between 900 and 1,000 died. Outside of London, the other city with equal density of population, it represented the highest single night's total for a European city until Dresden. Fifteen hundred people were injured, 400 of them seriously. Fifty-six thousand houses were damaged or destroyed, about half the city's stock of habitations, leaving 100,000 dwellers without shelter. When the raid began many instinctively stayed in their houses relying on the relative strength of the stairwell and the usual cupboard space 'under the stairs'. If the house was reasonably well built and did not suffer a direct hit by an HE its occupants usually survived. There are many recorded examples of survivors being dug alive out of the rubble of their homes. Not all were so lucky. Death could come from blast, incineration or shrapnel but more died from trauma from falling masonry. Thirty-five people took refuge in a mill in the Catholic New Lodge Road area, assuming that such a sturdy building would keep them safe. In a direct hit thirty-five people were killed, crushed when a wall fell on them. This was nearly as deadly an event as that which occurred when the towering side-wall of the York Street Spinning Mill fell on the tiny houses of Sussex Street and Vere Street.

The young Paddy Carolan was exhausted after his marathon walk about the bombed buildings of the Shore and Whitewell Roads and was less than gruntled when he was roused before eleven on the Tuesday evening. He was again refused shelter with his sister Bridie under the hearty (still-existing) table and was bundled into the glory hole again. There was no room for the father and he stayed on watch inside the house. The noise this time was too great for the Rosary to drown it but the astute Paddy soon persuaded the rest of the family that the steady repeated booming came not from the intermittent crash of bomb and landmine nor the hiss of scattering incendiaries but the shells (and shrapnel) from the ack-ack battery at Sunningdale at the top of the Cavehill Road. This ceased just before 2am when main communications were lost.

The bombs came quite close to the Carolan home in Marsden Gardens. Only 200 yards away a large house on the Antrim Road with extensive grounds belonging to a solicitor called McCleery avoided serious damage even after an HE device cratered the garden. One year later the families in that part of town had to be evacuated when a unexploded parachute landmine, one of Lord Haw-Haw's Easter eggs, was discovered in the Waterworks about the same distance away on the other side of the Cavehill Road. Catherwoods, a large builder's suppliers in Hopefield Avenue, less than 100 yards from the Carolan house, was hit and rendered no longer workable; it provided a dangerous but exciting adventure playground for the local children until rebuilding began after the war. They also scoured the streets for the bright silver shrapnel fragments that often had razor-sharp edges and soon rusted. The Catherwood bomb narrowly missed a girls orphanage further along Hopefield Avenue in the direction of the Waterworks. The two avenues north of Hopefield that like it, connected the Cavehill and the Antrim Roads, Cedar and Kansas, were also hit, and the noise, even in the glory hole, was horrendous. By the time the All Clear was sounding arrangements were already in train for the Carolan family evacuation. Not long before, in a house in Blythe Street, off Sandy Row, nearly two miles to the south, the Cairns family were huddled together under the stairs. A bomb fell close by and the whole stairway system was lifted by the blast and settled again. The then twelve-year-old Maudie Cairns clearly remembers that as their shelter rose a mouse ran out from underneath but escaped crushing as it scampered away to safety.

One of the observers of the carnage was Major Seán O'Sullivan of the Éire army, who was a kind of military attaché for de Valera's government. He arrived not long after the All Clear indicated by the ringing of handbells because there was no power to work the usual sirens. In his report prepared for the Dublin cabinet he noted:

> In the Antrim Road and vicinity the attack was of a particularly concentrated character and in many instances bombs from successive waves of bombers fell within 15–20 yards of one another... In this general area scores of houses were completely wrecked, either by explosion, fire or blast, while hundreds were damaged so badly as to be uninhabitable... In suburban areas many were allowed to burn themselves out and during the day wooden beams were still burning... During the night of 16–17, many of these smouldering fires broke out afresh and fire appliances could be heard passing throughout the night... It is estimated that the ultimate number of the dead may be in the neighbourhood of 500, and the final figures may even approach 2000.

He noted that in the areas of greatest bombing intensity the people had literally no idea how to protect themselves:

> In the heavily 'blitzed' areas people ran panic-stricken into the streets and made for the open country. As many were caught in the open by blast and secondary missiles, the enormous number of casualties can be readily accounted for. It is perhaps true that many saved their lives running but I am afraid a much greater number lost them or became casualties.

He praised the tireless heroism of the civil defence forces but realised that they were overwhelmed by the lack of a coherent protocol and the magnitude of the attack. No heavy cranes were available to shift rubble; rescue teams had to use pick and shovel and sometimes bare hands to rescue survivors trapped under broken masonry. One case he records was that of a child who had to have an arm and a leg amputated before extrication was possible. When he visited the Catholic Mater Hospital at the foot of the Crumlin Road at 2pm on Wednesday, 16 April he was shocked to see a traffic jam of ambulances waiting to deliver victims.

His informant was the Irish-Tasmanian, Thomas Theodore Flynn (1883–1968), the Professor of Zoology at Queen's since 1931, who had been appointed head of the casualty service for the city. Already vicariously famous as the father of the screen swashbuckler, Errol Flynn (1909–59), he was based at the Mater and gave O'Sullivan details of appalling casualties, 'due to shock, blast and secondary missiles, such as glass, stones, pieces of piping, etc'. O'Sullivan's report notes, 'There were many terrible mutilations among both living and dead – heads crushed, ghastly abdominal and face wounds, penetration by beams, mangled and crushed limbs…' His report ended with the thought that 'a second Belfast would be too horrible to contemplate'. Blast victims, as we have seen, often presented a more ghastly sight. When the city gasworks in Ormeau Road received a direct hit the utility exploded causing a temporary but fierce vacuum that drew all air, slates, windows and loose items out of the nearby houses. Inside the occupants lay unblemished but dead in their beds, eyes open in fear and mouths gaping in a desperate attempt to breathe.

Not all casualties were willing to be treated at the Mater. In *The Emperor of Ice Cream* (1965), the fifth novel by Belfast-born Brian Moore (1921–1999), he describes such a reluctant patient. The novel is the most clearly autobiographical of all Moore's work and it uses his experiences as an ARP worker during the big Blitz to paint a graphic picture of the time. His character, the twenty-year-old Gavin Burke, works for the Civil Defence organisation and his first client is an old woman, badly shocked and with a bleeding face:

> 'Shut up, mother,' Freddy said. 'Come on now we're nearly there.'
> 'Nearly where? Is it the papist hospital youse are taking me to?'
> 'Yes, mother,'

'Well youse can let me die in the street, so youse can. If you think I'm going to any Fenian hospital run by them nuns to get myself poisoned and kilt, then youse can have another think coming. Take me to the Royal Victoria, boys.'

Earlier she had claimed that it was 'the Fenians, the IRA' that had brought the Germans. As ever, in the hands of a skilled writer, fiction achieves a greater truth and a more shapely account of the confusion, the fear and the nausea of being on the front line.

Not all Protestants held out for treatment by those whom they believed they could trust. In the great 'fire-raid' of 4–5 May many women and children, who lived in the Shankill Road area, a location as firmly Protestant as Sandy Row, were relieved to find shelter in the crypt and cellar of Clonard Monastery that had been made ready to receive refugees after the experience of the raid of Holy Week. The impressive buildings, completed in 1911 for the monks of the Redemptorist Order, were sited off the Falls Road but close to what, during the later Troubles, would be known ironically as the 'peace line'. It was the obvious strongly built structure in the neighbourhood and when the afflicted people ran terrified from their collapsing and burning houses it was the place of refuge and hope. Most of the people who took shelter there had never been in a Catholic church before and the shared terror played its part in a brief reconciliation of the two usually warring sides. It was noted that the Protestant women and children led the singing of such hymns as Kethe's 'All People that on Earth Do Dwell', Winkworth's 'Now Thank We All Our God' and 'Praise to the Lord, the Almighty, the King of Creation', Lyte's 'Praise My Soul the King of Heaven' and 'Abide with Me', and Toplady's 'Rock of Ages'. One hymn not sung, for obviously psychological reasons, was Ellerton's 'The Day Thou Gavest, Lord, Is Ended'. These would not then have been heard at the time in Catholic churches though they are part of the hymnary now.

The terrible impersonal objectivity of the bombardiers as they aimed their missiles convinced most people that all were targets. The sense of shared horror as they made the walls of the Clonard resound could not but draw people together. Neighbours who were barely civil to each other became friends, and the sectarian violence of six years earlier now took on the character of a bad dream. The writer of one of the leaders in *The Irish Times* of Thursday, 17 April expressed a principle and a hope that could easily have affected a majority of the city's population:

> Humanity knows no borders, no politics, no differences of religious belief. Yesterday for once the people of Ireland were united under the shadow of a national blow. Has it taken bursting bombs to remind people of this little country that they have a common tradition, a common genius and a common home? Yesterday the hand of good-fellowship was reached across the Border. Men from the South worked with men from the North in the universal cause of the relief of suffering.

The same hitherto unheard of solidarity was to be reinforced when people of all classes took to 'ditching', leaving the city each evening at twilight to seek the safety of the surrounding hills. It was a splendid time for an official attempt at the reconciliation of the two opposed communities but Stormont had no statesmen of the calibre to take advantage of the heaven-sent if hell-born détente. Their main concern, expressed with their usual crassness, was to complain about the 'unbilletability' of the poor stricken refugees and express concern about the safety of Carson's statue.

In fact the Falls fared slightly better than the Shankill. One particularly savage incident was destruction of a shelter at the Shankill end of Percy Street that ran north from Divis Street. It was hit by a large parachute mine that caused such blast-suction that the walls of a crowded air-raid shelter crumpled exposing the people inside to blast damage. The heavy concrete roof was blown six feet away from the base and killed people where it fell and buried others in rubble. Sixty people in all were killed and of the rest some had to have legs amputated to free them from the debris. They were lucky in that a doctor from the district eventually arrived to do the grisly surgery. It was a typical example of the dangers of the 'open street'; death traps the small houses may have been, but they were safer than the blasted outside that was also exposed to shrapnel. Meanwhile the bombs continued to fall and victims were treated by amateur first-aid operators until professional medical help should arrive.

Nellie and Bob Bell, who had been married on Easter Monday, survived the raid, spending the night in a crowded shelter. The only honeymoon they could afford was a day trip to Bangor on Easter Tuesday. They had intended to start their married life together in Nellie's father's house in Crosscollyer Street, beside Alexandra Park in north Belfast. When the alert sounded they hastened to the house where the father was sitting reading with his feet in the hearth. His favourite author was Zane Grey (1875–1939), the Ohio dentist who had made a fortune writing authentic Western thrillers. Like most Belfast people of his age and time, having experienced many false alarms, he dismissed the threat implied in the sirens' call, saying, 'If there is a bomb with my name on it, I'll take it at my own fire side.' A bomb fell close by and the house shook. He reached for his boots and was half run, half carried by his daughter and new son-in-law to the shelter in nearby Deacon Street. The denizens passed the time in the total darkness by singing popular songs while an ARP warden stood on duty at the door. A plane flew very close to the street and he assured his charges that it was not a Luftwaffe bomber. Then recognising the halting note of the engine, he realised it was a German plane and they all began to sing 'Nearer My God to Thee'.

At dawn the Bells made their way back to the house in Crosscollyer Street to find it uninhabitable. As Nellie remembered it,

> …the sky was pink. I don't think it was just dawn… We were afraid to look round the corner as we came to our house. We couldn't imagine it would still be there, but there it was. The whole gable end was cracked and windows all broken and inside was awful. The few presents we got were buried under the glass and dirt from the bay window, which was caved in. Anything breakable was broken…

Her new husband was concerned about his mother who lived at the top of the Springfield Road and they set off to walk, as there was no public transport of any sort and no sign of taxis. As they moved down the Antrim Road they passed by the shelter that had suffered a direct hit and they watched mutely as the dead and injured were being carried out. Like all eyewitnesses of the catastrophe they were appalled and upset at the numbers of the casualties and the sight of their broken bodies.

The Phoenix Bar was still standing, if without doors or windows, and a necessary drink gave them the strength to continue through the desolate city. The Bell family were unhurt and the house untouched, and in sheer hysteria produced by shock, fear, cold and lack of sleep, Nellie broke down and continued to weep until her mother-in-law upbraided her. It was probably a necessary short sharp shock but it was a poor beginning for the third day of a young bride's married life. 'I took a long time to forgive her for barging me as she did. I was only married after all. All my dreams and hopes and we didn't know what more was going to happen.' It was the fear of 'what more was going to happen' that caused them and thousands of their fellow citizens to find a rural haven away from the battered city. They sheltered for a while in a shared cottage at Donacloney near Banbridge, County Down. Bob, who worked shifts 6.00 to 2.00 and 2.00 to 10.00, had to make his way each day into town to work. For the first shift he had to rise at about 3am and walk the four or five miles to Lurgan where he got the train to Belfast. The other shift was not much better since it meant leaving the cottage at 11 o'clock in the morning. When the Bells felt the danger had lessened they moved back to Belfast to a flat above a pub in North Queen Street and spent the next fourteen years there before being rehoused.

So cataclysmic an event was not without its share of anecdotes, impossible to verify, but not unlikely in the circumstances. One was crudely sectarian: a pork butcher's store in York Street received a direct hit from an HE bomb and the story flew round that once its owner had displayed a carcase in the window saying, 'This pig was cured at Lourdes.' Another tale was of a notorious backstreet moneylender from the Shankill Road area who flew to the shelter carrying a cat under her arm. When she was complimented on her tenderness to her pet, she looked and swore, 'I thought it was my cash bag.'

The city's main theatres were working as usual. The Grand Opera House had the Savoy Players, the resident repertory company, present *The Passing of the Third Floor Back* (1908) during Holy Week. The play by Jerome K Jerome (1857–1929), author of the comic success *Three Men in a Boat* (1898), deals with the visit of a mysterious Christ-like figure that has a remarkable effect on the lives of the inhabitants of a London boarding-house and was thought appropriate for the season. The offering for Easter Week was 'the funniest of all farces', *It's a Boy*, adapted from a 1934 British film. The Empire had a revue called – what else? – *April Showers*. But it was the production in the little Group Theatre of the perennially popular Belfast play, *Boyd's Shop* (1936) by St John Ervine (1883–1971), that attracted the most enthusiastic audiences and sold out the theatre each evening. So popular was the play that one very pious lady was persuaded to make her first ever visit to a theatre to see it. She later decided that the raid was a personal punishment upon her for going to such an immoral institution. The Group staged their plays in the Minor Ulster Hall and the star attraction in the main hall that night was the remarkable ballad singer Delia Murphy (1902–71), wife of Thomas Kiernan, the Irish ambassador to the Vatican and later Canada. When the sirens sounded she went on singing and persuaded the audience to stay in the building. They joined her in the choruses of 'If I Were a Blackbird', 'Moonlight in Mayo' and 'The Moonshiner' and in fact remained safe since no HE bombs fell in Bedford Street.

The perceived imbalance in bomb, incendiary and mine distribution confirmed in the minds of the ultra-bigoted that the raids were somehow targeted only at Protestant areas at the behest of the pope. In fact the raid of Holy Week had been concentrated on the docks, shipyards and engineering works where the workforce were mainly Protestant and, from the very beginnings of the industrialisation of the city, their dwellings were built close to the works. There were, too, many more Protestant churches in Belfast than Catholic, catering for a wide spectrum of varying beliefs. Since the IRA, by then moribund thanks to internment in the north and an even more absolute campaign by de Valera's government, had been seen to burn respirators when they were first issued extremists had no difficulty in believing the most extreme rumours, including the utterly surreal suggestion that the pope was in the cockpit of the leading bomber, guiding the plane away from Catholic areas and towards Protestant ones. The remark was taken by most people to be a metaphor but some of the lunatic fringe may have actually believed it. The prospect of the austere sixty-five-year-old Eugenio Pacelli, in flying-suit and goggles, pointing towards the Shankill, stretches even the most elastic imagination.

The morning of Wednesday, 16 April revealed the extent of the damage but the death toll and the roster of the injured took longer to count. There were for example a number of bodies that were never identified. Perhaps some of them were members of the same family and had no one surviving to identify them. Others were the solitaries, loners, drop-outs, the *Dreck* of an urban sprawl with an almost non-existent welfare system. Those identifiable as Catholics, by such items as rosary beads or scapulars, were buried in a mass grave in Milltown Cemetery, with a large gravestone inscribed: 'Sacred to the memory of unidentified victims of enemy action. Belfast, April 1941.' An equivalent memorial stone marks the mass grave in the City Cemetery on the Falls Road for those not designated. Lists of the identified dead were compiled at the various mortuaries where the bodies were displayed. Some of these were adjuncts of professional funeral parlours like those of the firms of Melville and Johnson (Wilton's, on the Crumlin Road, one of the largest of these, had been reduced to a shell); most were part of hospital complexes, including the Royal

Victoria, the Belfast Union at the City, the Ulster at Dundonald, the Belfast Hospital for Sick Children on the Falls Road, and the Mater, probably closest to the destruction. The lists of the identified dead compiled by the Civil Defence Authority also contained their addresses. The frequent recurrence of certain streets – Ballynure (sixteen dead, nine from one family), Disraeli (ten dead), Vere and Sussex (thirty-five dead), Ohio (twenty-nine dead), Percy (sixty dead), Hogarth (forty-five dead), Lincoln Avenue (ten dead), Veryan Gardens (forty-six dead), and, of course, York Street, on the front line – gave a kind of intensity table of destruction.

At least the display of bodies in hospitals and in the small Belfast Mortuary on Laganbank Road was clinical and professional but there was simply not enough space. To accommodate fatalities much in excess of the city's emergency capacity the swimming bath on the Falls Road was drained and the large covered St George's Market at the foot of May Street requisitioned as extra mortuaries. At first those officials in charge of body disposition had used the tiled edges of the swimming pool to lay out the corpses until all the available space was used and then, as the numbers grew, the water was removed. The bodies, mainly from the York Street and Percy Street carnage, were brought to the sites by any requisitionable transport that included furniture vans, coal lorries and even Corporation bin-lorries. Eventually the store of coffins ran out and the corpses were left as they were found, some wrapped in blankets, some naked. One young lad of fifteen who had volunteered to help in the Falls Road had his first acquaintance with corpses and had never seen a naked woman before. The effect on him was profound.

Brian Moore was just twenty and his experiences in the Mater mortuary hardened him to the cruelties of war. (At least, so he thought, until he visited Auschwitz.) His hero Gavin Burke in *The Emperor of Ice Cream* is a composite version of the author in his family background, his intermittent lust and his relative inexperience both of the facts of real life and the rawly sectarian nature of his native city. All of these themes are dealt with in the book in the author's usual deft way. His description of the shame, the pity and the meaninglessness of such slaughter remains the best summary of the Wednesday morning after the raid – even here in the relative order of the mortuary in the Mater:

> In the stink of human excrement, in the acrid smell of disinfectant these dead were heaped, body on body, flung arm, twisted feet, open mouth, staring eyes, old men on top of young women, a child lying on a policeman's back, a soldier's hand resting on a woman's thigh, a carter still wearing his coal-slacks on top of a pile of arms and legs, his own arm outstretched, finger pointing as though he warned of some unseen horror. Forbidding and clumsy, the dead cluttered the morgue room from floor to ceiling.

Even more chilling was Moore's contribution to a BBC documentary, *No Survivors in Burke Street* (1991):

> I was walking up Tennent Street towards Carlisle Circus... I suddenly looked to the left and I saw what looked like a hundred rats which had come up from the sewers and were going in a kind of procession along the edge of the gutters, not on the pavement, going up towards Carlisle Circus, not fast, just moving slowly. That was the most frightening thing to me that I'd seen.

There is a slight irony in that Burke Street itself did not survive, having been part of an extensive redevelopment in the region of North Queen Street.

One very valuable source for the events of that Easter Week is *Post 381: The Memoirs of a Belfast Air Raid Warden* (1989) by James Doherty. He was young and vigorous but what he experienced made such an impression that his memoirs read as if the events he describes had happened only the previous week. He and some fellow members of the ARP had left Delia Murphy's concert in spite of the risk and the last he saw of his companions was the moment when they said goodbye and made their way up to their post in Clifton Street. They could not have known that already a deadly parachute mine had begun its drift down on to their station and all were killed. Doherty had earlier observed that the drive to make the blackout perfect was utterly pointless as he saw the parts of the city lit up by flares and incendiaries. He was becoming used to the horrors, of bodies turned into cooked meat by bomb blast. He knew the people of Percy Street and was aware that one of the girls who lived there rather fancied him. Unfortunately she was one of the casualties when the shelter sustained a direct hit. Among the ghastly events that he found unforgettable was the finding in rubble of the blonde head of a young woman and a boy's sock with a foot in it. Young as he was he volunteered for duty at the Falls Baths, where the main swimming pool that he knew well as a swimmer now fulfilled a different purpose:

> It was about 8am when we arrived. We expected a similar scene to that at the Mater Hospital where relatives were milling around searching for news of families or friends. This morning there were no crowds and comparatively few people. On our way in the first shock of the morning was the sight of a burnt hand lying in the doorway but there were more to come. We had volunteered but we were totally unprepared for the real horror that was to follow. Hundreds of bodies brought in from scattered incidents were lying all around us. They were men and women, young people, children and infants. How could anyone have visualised seeing so many broken bodies in one place? No textbooks, no training pamphlets could have prepared us for the grim task we were about to undertake. Some were whole and others hardly resembled human beings… Any information that could help us identify the unfortunate victims was recorded. Watches, rings, photographs and other personal effects were listed to help with identification. Details of where bodies were found were not always useful in establishing identity. In many cases they were killed on their way home and they were found in areas far from their own districts and among strangers. Bodies were laid out in plain box-like coffins. Mothers and infants were laid out together just as they had been found. We could imagine a mother clutching her baby close to her as the bombs fell. The baths were intended to be used as a mortuary where people could go to identify the dead but it became too crowded. The baths were drained and the bodies were put down on to the tiled floor of the pool but more and more of them came in. The air was filled with the stench of dead bodies and a heavy concentration of disinfectant. Some of the workers took sick…

Emma Duffin, one of the volunteers at St George's Market, who had been a VAD nurse in France and Egypt during the Great War, twenty-five years previously, kept a diary at the time, now preserved in an archive in the Public Records Office of Northern Ireland (PRONI). One entry describes a visit to the site on the Saturday afternoon of 19 April:

> It was a job for an older woman and my experience at the hospital should have prepared me to some extent... The place was full of coffins... Red Cross and St John ambulance nurses and some civilians met and went around with relatives. Two men went around with each group and opened the coffins, lifting the lids... A man watered the floor with disinfectant from a watering pail; a wise precaution as the place smelt. All the way to the place I told myself I was bound to see horrible sights but only when seen could the full horror be realised. I had seen many dead but they had died in hospital beds, their eyes had been reverently closed, their hands crossed on their breasts: death had, to a certain extent, been glossed over, made decent. It was solemn, tragic, dignified. Here it was grotesque, repulsive, horrible... With tangled hair, staring eyes, clutching hands, contorted limbs, their grey green faces covered with dust they lay bundled into coffins, half-shrouded in rugs or blankets or an occasional sheet, still wearing their dirty torn twisted garments... I felt outraged, I should have felt sympathy, grief, but instead feelings of revulsion and disgust assailed me.

Two hundred and fifty-five bodies were displayed in the market in the hope that relatives, searching for the missing, might be able to identify them. To prevent voyeurism only a few visitors were allowed in at a time. In spite of this some people from other parts of Ulster travelled to the city to see for themselves the extent of the damage. Some of them could not resist attempting to look at the latter-day charnel houses but the majority regretted their morbid curiosity. Because of the time of year and the delay in burial the bodies were at different stages of decomposition. This fact and the awful injuries visible upon the corpses made identification increasingly more difficult. Further, the market though spacious and covered was not rodent-proof. It was decided that remains not identified by Monday,

21 April should be buried anyway. For urgent reasons of hygiene and because the stench of decomposition was beginning to sicken even the most resolute of the Civil Defence officials, the bodies were taken from the Falls Baths and St George's Market, those from the former in even more nauseating condition, and laid out on the grass in May's Fields, then open ground beside the Lagan. There too were placed the broken pieces of bodies, green with rot, that were revealed as the workers cleared up the seemingly endless piles of rubble. It is not recorded how many visitors, anxious to be reassured or dreading that their worse fears might be confirmed, faced the noisome prospect of visiting the temporary necropolis. The sight of a rota of ARP volunteers continually hosing the poor mangled remains to delay the decomposition process, must have added to the nightmarish horror of a city in the grip of bewildered dysfunction.

On the Monday the 163 unclaimed or unidentified bodies were taken in plain wooden coffins by army lorries to the appropriate resting places. A procession of nurses and ARP personnel in uniform followed for lack of ordinary mourners. The cortege made its way up the Falls Road to the top of Donegall Road, where those thought to be Protestant were buried in a single grave in the City Cemetery while the rest identified as Catholic by Rosary beads, holy medals and other religious paraphernalia continued up the road to Milltown. The final casualty figures are still a matter of some dispute. Lists were published in local papers, the names running to three full columns in the Saturday *Belfast Telegraph*. The unidentified bodies were dealt with in seemly dispatch but the private funerals of nearly 900 bodies filled the Falls Road with frequent hearses as the bereaved followed their loved ones through crowded streets. Bystanders lost count as the seemingly endless procession clattered on.

Sir John Maffey (1877–1969), the popular but sorely tried British ambassador to Éire, was in Belfast that morning and reported later to de Valera that the scenes he witnessed were 'more horrifying than London because of the numbers of small dwelling houses of poor people that were destroyed'. It was the condition of the fabric of these relics of Belfast's industrial revolution and their logical proximity to the giant workplaces that compounded the slaughter. A report published in December 1941, when there were still many official and unofficial refugees, concluded that the likely number of occupants of a terrace house was fifteen. When a stick of HEs fell in a street it literally tore the dwellings apart. In his magisterial account of the Belfast raids, *The Blitz* (1989), Brian Barton quotes a newspaper report that describes how roofs were lifted and bodies hurled from inside their homes, tossed into neighbouring streets. A significant contribution to the death toll in working-class areas was this combination of weak structure and crowded living conditions. The understandable hesitation about making use of the inadequate and insecure shelter provision added to the fear and confusion of the city that week and saw the greatest instant and spontaneous folk movement in Belfast's history.

6

'Up the Dubs!'

IT WAS PROBABLY AROUND 1.30AM ON Wednesday, 16 April that John MacDermott asked the Dublin operator to connect him with the Taoiseach's residence to seek help in fighting the fires that raged in Belfast. It was at the same time the most logical possible act and the least likely, considering MacDermott's firm Unionist stance and the mixture of mockery and resentment with which his government viewed de Valera's insistence on Éire's neutrality.

MacDermott was younger than most of his cabinet colleagues, forty-five then, and much more gifted if no less adamantine in his defence of partition and distrust of southern politicians. He was, too, much more pragmatic and took his responsibilities as Minister of Home Security very seriously. The city was in trouble and its own fire services were unable to cope with the damage wrought by the 29,000 incendiary bombs and 200,000 tons of HEs that were devastating its populace. The fire service was clearly inadequate to deal with the situation, the crisis intensified by the inadequacy of central control. It is likely that no service, however efficient, could have dealt with the situation that Easter but the Belfast brigade seems to have been just about adequate for peacetime purposes and totally unprepared for the reality of modern war. The widespread optimism that Belfast would never be bombed combined with official complacency had had dire consequences.

A Brigade District Officer had earlier risked writing directly to MacDermott's department drawing attention to the firmly held belief among the rank and file that the service was not at all able to deal with a major incident. The top brass closed ranks and suggested that the whistleblower be disciplined but he was vindicated by a report presented in March 1941 that confirmed the accuracy of his observations. Two hundred and fifty new full-time fire-fighters were to be recruited and four new stations built. No response had been made by Easter 1941 and then, heroic as individual fire-fighters proved to be, there were not enough of them. Ruptured gas mains added their own flames, and because of the concentration of HEs on the Waterworks, pressure throughout central and north Belfast was drastically reduced. The gas supply, then the main source of street lighting and cooking, was cut off from most of the city. Though 200 appliances were active the bombing had caused many major fractures of mains so that water had to be cut off completely in the Greencastle, Antrim Road and Cavehill Road areas. Another source of water, the tidal Lagan as it flowed into the lough, was fuller than it had been eight days before but there was a shortage of pumping equipment, as of much else thanks to the complacent optimism of the cabinet.

It is thought that it was RD Harrison, City Commissioner of Police, who suggested to MacDermott that he should ask de Valera for help. It was a daring idea and the two people in question had to make swift, problematic, and, for each, reluctant decisions. MacDermott was giving recognition to a leader whose existence the Northern Ireland government barely admitted; de Valera ran the risk of having his neutral stance severely and publicly compromised. Still neither hesitated, though they afterwards played down the drama of the occasion. MacDermott could never quite remember which government official he first spoke to and there is apparently no archival material either in Stormont or the Dáil relating to the event. Dr

Christopher McGimpsey in his introduction to the facsimile edition (1984) of the collection of photographs of bomb damage, published in 1941 and called *Bombs on Belfast*, states that a telegram was sent to the Town Clerk of Dublin at 4.30am 'asking that southern brigades help fight the Belfast fires' and that by 6.00am the message came that aid was on its way. Decent obscurity seems to have been the watchword.

According to Sean Redmond, whose monograph *Belfast is Burning* (2002) gives an account of the incident from the southern point of view, Major JJ Comerford, Dublin's Chief Fire Officer, arrived at the service's headquarters in Tara Street, famous for its Florentine tower, at about 2.30am on Wednesday morning. This was so unusual as to cause speculation because Comerford rarely appeared outside of normal daytime hours. Something major had clearly happened. He sought thirty volunteers who would go north to help in the desperate struggle to control the inferno. He got his volunteers without difficulty and they were already past Whitehall on the Belfast road by 5.00am to be joined on the way by colleagues from brigades from Dún Laoghaire, Drogheda and Dundalk. If they thought about the situation at all it was just that they were fire-fighters on another 'shout' and were not concerned with politics, local or international. Comerford had been able to reassure them that should the worst occur their families would be taken care of. Thirteen appliances and ambulances crossed at the Killeen border post between Dundalk and Newry. As one of the travellers remarked, 'There was no border that night.' Already they could see the red glare of the fires light up the skies. It was the only light they had because of the blackout, and they kept on the right road by following the telegraph wires. It was bitterly cold, they remembered; the Dennis appliances had only the system of ladders as roofs, otherwise they were open. They went straight to the Belfast headquarters in Chichester Street and, seasoned as they were to disaster, they were appalled by what they had already seen on the road in from Lisburn.

The Dún Laoghaire contingent consisted of one officer, five crew and two volunteers from the Éire auxiliary fire service. Their vehicle was also an open Dennis with no shelter except a windscreen to protect the driver, and the night was clear and frosty. One of them, Edward Lennon, recalls seeing lorries as they passed St George's Market loaded with corpses being taken for display and identification. The southern fire-fighters fought the blaze all day long on the Wednesday and did not head for home until midnight. One of the Dublin appliances broke down and had to be towed home by a Dún Laoghaire engine. The early edition of the *Belfast Telegraph* of Thursday, 17 April mentioned the 'splendid help from the Dublin fire service, who reached the Ulster capital after a three hour dash' and in its editorial commented upon 'the magnificent spirit which prompted fire brigades to rush to the assistance of their comrades in the North. This is the good neighbour spirit in action.' Both these comments need deconstruction; the praise was lavish but entirely within the wary condition of 'them' and 'us'. The phrase 'Ulster capital' speaks volumes.

The southern firemen were appalled by the waste of dead bodies of humans and animals strewn about. One ran up a Belfast fire engine ladder to rescue a hose from a burning building and then realised just in time that the ladder was the only support of the building that collapsed as soon as they moved it away. Much attention was paid to the burning wreck of the Belfast Rope Works. The Belfast firemen wanted that fire to be quenched before blackout, which would then have been about 9.00 that evening. They feared that the Luftwaffe would come again that night and with so many fires still raging they would have had no need of flares. Fortunately this did not happen. Some of the Dublin contingent were only mildly shocked when they came upon looters in a blazing public house at the corner of Chichester Street. These 'local entrepreneurs' did not depart when the hoses began to play; they simply requested that the Dubs should cool down the pub's safe that was still too hot to touch. Brian Barton notes that so great was the confusion in the city that when some of the Dublin firemen arrived they reported to Lisburn Road police station but waited for two hours before they were assigned to particular conflagrations. Though the visitors worked all day there was no provision made to feed them and without ration books there was little they could buy in the shops that were still open. Each was later given five shillings for the dinner they missed. The Drogheda contingent, assigned to the area at the foot of High Street near the Albert Clock, fared slightly better. Those dockers able to go to work shared their 'pieces' with them, though the lunches consisted mainly of 'doorstoppers' of bread filled with slices of raw onion.

All the southern firemen, having tackled fires of magnitude and intensity that they had never seen before, or would see afterwards, had gone home before midnight, it is now felt, deliberately. The international complications of neutral firemen being fatalities in the enemy country of the United Kingdom could well have caused a flurry in the Reichstag. Still, when the Luftwaffe did return on 4–5 May to saturate Belfast with incendiaries and ignite the Great Fire of Belfast, thirteen appliances and ambulances from the same four Leinster brigades made the journey north again. This time considerations of neutrality and local politics were ignored. There was no complicated use of intermediaries; at 2.00am on the morning of 5 May Ben Smith, the new Chief Fire Officer in Belfast, rang Tara Street and help was on its way without hesitation.

The two journeys assumed some of the characteristics of an epic and, like all epics, they attracted by accretion some potent myths. One story was that the appliances arrived into central Belfast with green, white and orange tricolours flying from each. The story could have originated with either tradition – or both. Nationalists could have floated it as the Irish equivalent of the cod assertion: 'Never in the history of motion pictures has the United States cavalry ever been late.' Belfast was in dire straits and here were sound men with southern accents coming to its rescue. With Unionists it might have seemed that these were decent lads coming to help, but the rescuers couldn't even for a moment forget their relentless Republicanism. In fact the story was completely untrue; the last things that the firemen were thinking of as they raced in some trepidation northwards were flags and emblems. The other myth, almost certainly devised by the nationalist community, was that the Irish crews spent their times in the 'Ulster capital' fighting fires in the Protestant Shankill Road; again it was just a story but as *Il Duce* might have said, '*Se non è vero, è molto ben trovato.*' All the rules of romance and drama demand that it be true. What *was* true was best described in a rare example of emotion in an otherwise very sober book by John W Blake in his official history, *Northern Ireland in the Second World War* (1956): 'Help came at once from Eire, and Ulstermen will long remember the cheering sight of thirteen fire engines from Dublin, Drogheda, Dundalk and Dun Laoghaire (Kingstown) speeding through the night on their errand of mercy with full lights blazing.' The bracketed 'Kingstown' was for the benefit of those still living in the year 1921.

Another tale of the time was that Alfie Byrne (1882–1956), the son of a docker who went on to serve as Lord Mayor of Dublin from 1930 to 1939, and again in 1954–5, had travelled north in one of the appliances. Byrne was one of the best-known characters in the Dublin of the 1930s, '40s and '50s. He was dubbed 'the shaking hand of Dublin', not in any pathological sense, but because of his ubiquity, his friendliness and his readiness to offer his hand to perfect strangers. The unlikely claim was made for him that he had shaken the hand of every man, woman and child in the city. An independent MP (the last of the old Irish Parliamentary Party) and an independent TD from 1922 until his death (with a short break in the Senate), he was better known than most of the reigning Fianna Fáil cabinet, and literature demands as a kind of epic imperative that he take part in the events of some of Dublin's finest hours. The story of his riding on the Dublin appliances is, to say the least of it, unlikely if not spurious. 'Elfan Safetee' rules were not as draconian as they have since become in the compensation culture of the twenty-first century but they did exist. The position of the professional fire-fighters was problematic enough in the matter of insurance coverage, to say nothing of safety considerations.

It is hardly conceivable that Comerford could have permitted a civilian, however colourful and charismatic, to travel on one of the appliances. The story, however, still persists as part of the oral folklore of the time. Though there is no other evidence for its having happened, there is something very appealing in the thought of the neat, dapper, moustachioed fifty-nine-year-old riding shotgun in an open Dennis, dressed in his accustomed black frock coat and formal cutaway collar. In Douglas Carson's BBC NI radio programme, *The Belfast Blitz*, broadcast on 22 November 1973, one of the voices is that of a fireman remembering: 'It was very cold and I nearly froze driving that open engine to Belfast. I had to sit on my hands to keep them from getting numb. There were no landmarks on the way up; we reached our destination by following the telephone lines…' If Byrne did manage the journey it was an appropriate part of his colourful life story. Byrne's name does appear in one of the few relevant documents that have survived. An *Irish Press* account of a meeting of the Dublin Corporation on 23 April notes his recommendation that the matter of insurance and payment be referred to the General Purposes Committee. Sean Redmond suggests that since he still had the status of an alderman and TD he may have 'made a symbolic gesture of travelling on an appliance to perhaps the city boundary'.

One anecdote of the time has the air of authenticity. One family who had wisely taken refuge under the stairs were completely buried when the house collapsed on top of them. They had shouted for a long time without effect and then were relieved to hear digging above them. They renewed their shouting and were delighted to be answered from above but in an odd accent. The rescuers, following standard procedure, kept talking to the trapped family until finally with the removal of a brick they could see light and realised that the uniforms were oddly different. The father asked, 'Who are you?' and got the answer, 'We are the Dublin fire brigade.' He replied with typical deadpan Belfast wit, 'It must have been a mighty bomb – we've been blown all the way from Belfast to Dublin.'

The whole affair remains clouded in apparently deliberate obfuscation. Relevant documents were either shredded or did not exist. Looking back with all the wariness of a society hounded by political correctness and Elfan Safetee considerations one must admit that the episode bristled with procedural difficulties. In spite of all temptations to play safe the Éire authorities were bold and generous. One document from the city council archives in Dublin, printed as an appendix in Sean Redmond's monograph, gives a sequence of the events of the night of the Great Fire, 5 May 1941, as recorded by PJ Hernon, the Dublin City Manager and Town Clerk. It begins: '12.30am – Taoiseach phoned and said that Belfast had again been attacked. Told me to be prepared to send assistance if called upon to do so.' Hernon phoned Comerford to alert him ten minutes later. De Valera rang again at 12.45 advising that the brigade should travel in daylight if possible, but if an urgent message were received they 'should have to take the risk and go'. At 2.25 de Valera rang again to commandeer all available fire assistance for the trip to Belfast. The guards and defence forces were to be informed so that the way could be cleared for the appliances and ambulances. He also said that they were to confine their activities 'to rescue from private houses rather than military objectives'. At 3.40 Comerford rang Hernon to say that thirteen Dublin firemen had gone on two vehicles and eleven were about to start on two more. One crew each from Dún Laoghaire, Drogheda and Dundalk were on the way north, and two Auxiliary Fire crews from Tara Street. Hernon had to advise the Taoiseach that 'in the case of accident to the men legislation would have to be introduced to deal with the matter'.

In all twenty-five regular and twenty-nine auxiliaries were sent, roughly twice the number that had attended in April. Even so Superintendent Gorman, the fireman in charge of the volunteers in

Belfast, sent a message at 7.00am: 'Fires out of control. Send seventeen men and one pump.' Another document printed in *Belfast is Burning* are notes written in Hernon's hand on the back of an envelope that returns to the troublesome matter of insurance for the Irish AFS and probably followed on from de Valera's phone calls. What follows is exactly what was jotted down:

> Request humanitarian grounds and could not refuse. Felt certain. Sent with government approval volunteers in case of accident quite certain if necessary legislation passed to compensate in case of accident. I feel certain that if were necessary the Government would introduce legislation enabling compensation to be paid and he felt certain that the State would on this occasion should it arise face up to its responsibilities on this matter. Minister for Finance wants it to be understood no commitment to pay all cost.

The ever-watchful Minister for Finance was Sean MacEntee (1889–1984), doing what such ministers have to do. The document has its own drama, balancing need with practical difficulties but there was never any doubt that heart would win over head.

If such a list of phone calls had existed for the night of 16 April much of the obscurity could have been dispelled and many contradictions reconciled. One expects that such documentation must have existed but researchers have been so far unable to access it. Certainly the only clarity about the earlier Belfast venture was about the readiness and the heroism of the volunteers. The political implications are of interest only to historians and all from the most virid of green to the most mandarin of orange applauded the actions on both the occasions. One of the reasons for the tactical obscurity is rooted in Éire's neutrality. History has shown that de Valera's government, though formally neutral, tended to find itself on the side of the Allies, especially when the United States entered the war after the attack by the Japanese on Pearl Harbour on 7 December 1941. The British and Irish intelligence services cooperated closely, meteorological information about Atlantic weather was sent regularly to the British Air Ministry, Allied servicemen who found themselves

The terraced housing of Annadale Street, as in so many other working-class streets in the city, was devastated as a consequence of the Luftwaffe's "Easter eggs" delivered on the night of 15–16 April, 1941.

A surreal vision of Hughenden Avenue in the aftermath of the Easter Tuesday raid.

As part of a morale-boosting visit to the city, the Duke and Duchess of Gloucester are seen here inspecting the air raid damage inflicted on Percy Street.

Members of the Auxiliary Fire Service in action in York Street, one of the worst affected areas in the Blitz.

Belfast became a city of wrecked churches as a result of the carnage, as shown here by the stark remains of Newington Presbyterian Church on the Limestone Road.

Many children were evacuated from the city as a result of the Easter raid. The sense of adventure evident in this group of youngsters is at odds with the concern on the faces of the adults.

A picture of wartime spirit amid the death and destruction in April: an organist performs an impromptu musical interlude at the top of Jennymount Street.

The changed face of the Bridge Street and High Street area after the May raid.

The Great Fire of Belfast: a fireman battles heroically against the flames in Castle Lane on the night of 4–5 May.

A sentry witnesses the demolition of Hazlett's in North Street in the wake of the Belfast firestorm.

The main damage to the City Hall was centred on the Banquet Room which was left stripped of its former magnificence.

The twisted stern-framing of a corvette in Harland & Wolff stands on the edge of a massive crater after the German attack on Belfast's industrial heartland, 15–16 April, 1941.

in Éire's territory were tactfully hushed back across the border, and there existed a permitted air corridor in Donegal that was used by Allied planes operating out of County Fermanagh.

It took a statesman of supreme funambulatory talent like de Valera to permit these relaxations in strict neutrality and he had to be careful in his relations with Dr Eduard Hempel, the German Minister. He had flagged his attitude on 31 August 1939 when Hempel informed him that Joachim von Ribbentrop (1893–1946), the German Foreign Minister, had assured him that Germany would respect Éire's neutrality. He replied that though Éire desired peace with all nations including Germany, she should have to show some consideration to Britain for economic and geographical reasons. It helped that Hempel was a career diplomat and not a Nazi but de Valera still had to walk a tightrope. His notorious visit to the German Legation on 30 April 1945 to sympathise with Hempel on the announced suicide of Hitler was mainly a tribute to the legate's impeccable behaviour during the war and of course another adamantine proof of Éire's absolute neutrality. The call for help by whatever means mediated required an instant and agonising decision and he did not hesitate.

Without relevant papers it is difficult to state what actually happened on the fateful April Wednesday. Most of the sparse evidence is contradictory when collated with the few documents available. MacDermott was vague, perhaps diplomatically so, about what time he rang Dublin and to whom he asked to speak to about the emergency. One-thirty am, the time he suggests in his interview with Robert Fisk, the author of *In Time of War*, the standard work of the history of Ireland during the war, would seem to have been confirmed by the time of the visit of Comerford to Tara Street and the belief by several biographers that de Valera was roused at 2.00am. This cannot be reconciled with the suggestion that Harrison did not get in touch with MacDermott until 4.30.

One other significant player in the drama is Cardinal Joseph MacRory (1861–1945), Archbishop of Armagh and Primate of All

Ireland. He remained a vocal critic of the Stormont regime especially when he was Bishop of Down and Connor but he was conscious of his responsibility for his flock on both sides of the border. He was foremost in leading the nationalist campaigns against conscription and, in a sense, was the political as well as the ecclesiastical leader of Northern Catholics. There is some oral evidence that he was involved in the decision to send the men to Belfast. Redmond quotes one of the Tara Street firemen as remembering Comerford saying on his first appearance at the headquarters, 'The Primate has spoken to Dev about the bombing and Dev is asking us to help.'

It is possible that MacDermott decided that MacRory was the best, because safest, intermediary between Belfast and Dublin. He was deeply concerned with the welfare of all his people but his archdiocese of Armagh, though it included County Louth, was mainly in Northern Ireland. He could not have been unaware of the raid. If the travelling firemen could see a pall of smoke over the crimson and yellow glow above the city from Newry he could see it equally well from the primatial city. MacDermott's priority was help for the stricken city but he was too much of a politician not to be aware of what a request from Dublin might mean politically. He had, of course, asked for help from the nearest British cities, Liverpool and Glasgow. They responded but could not arrive until the Thursday afternoon when a total of forty-two pumps were sent across the narrow sea. As a Protestant normally suspicious and essentially ignorant of the way Catholicism actually worked, MacDermott may have been influenced by his party's belief that Éire was a priest-run state, taking orders from Rome through its leading churchman. He was judicious enough not to involve his own prime minister, the weak and vacillating John M Andrews, but rather alerted his deputy and eventual successor, Sir Basil Brooke, who recorded in his diary that he had given approval for the request. It was a sleepless night for all concerned but there seems little doubt that for as long as telephonic communication was possible MacRory had been in constant touch with de Valera.

The Dublin papers, perhaps by Government direction, were almost non-committal. The only reference in the full three-column coverage of the raid by the *Irish Independent* on 17 April was the single sentence: 'Units of fire fighting and ambulance services from some of the towns in the Twenty Six counties assisted in putting out fires resulting from the raids.' Frank Aiken (1898–1983), the Minister of Defence, was ultimately responsible for the removal of any material that could be interpreted as 'propaganda' for either Allies or Axis. Many films, especially those with wartime themes, were banned and no word of praise or criticism of either side permitted. Even a number of the series of fourteen Sherlock Holmes films made in the 1940s with Basil Rathbone (1892–1967) and Nigel Bruce (1895–1953), the best ever characterisations of the famous Baker Street detectives, were not permitted to be shown. Their titles, *Sherlock Holmes and the Voice of Fear* (1941) and *Sherlock Holmes and the Secret Weapon* (1942), were enough to damn them. It was not until *The Scarlet Claw* (1944), set safely in Canada, with no mention of the Germans, that these innocuous films began to be shown again. The attitude of the Dublin censors was in fact replicated instinctively among northern nationalists and though the films were not censored they were dubbed 'propaganda' and often boycotted.

The *Irish Press* of 17 April had the same scant coverage and one can only guess at the frustrations felt by the editors in not being able to follow up such marvellous human interest stories. No returning fire-fighters were interviewed and much good information was lost. Late on the afternoon of the same day the Dublin newsboys with their usual cries of 'Hegler Mail' sold copies of the *Evening Herald* and the *Evening Mail* that covered the bombing. Neither paper made any mention of the involvement of the southern services. Clearly their editors had had a visit from the censors before the papers went to press. The staff of the government censorship office were described by RM Smyllie (1894–1954), then the charismatic editor of *The Irish Times* and a constant sufferer at their hands, as 'troglyditic myrmidons, moronic clodhoppers, ignorant bosthoons, poor cawbogues whose only claim to literacy was their blue pencils'. At the time, Aiken was in the United States, then still neutral, and when asked by American reporters about the involvement of his fire services, said tersely, 'Of course we should go to Belfast. They are Irish people too.' De Valera was in Castlebar on 19 April, a few days after the Blitz, to address representatives of the parish councils of County Mayo. His own paper, the *Press*, printed his speech on 20 April:

> This is the first time I have spoken in public since the disaster in Belfast and I know you will all wish me to express on your behalf, and on behalf of the government, our sympathy with the people who are suffering there. In the past, and probably in the present too, a number of them did not see eye to eye with us politically but they are all our people – we are one and the same people – and their sorrows in the present instance are also our sorrows, and I want to say that any help we can give them in the present time we will give them wholeheartedly, believing that were the circumstances reversed they would also give us their support wholeheartedly.

The story was reprinted approvingly the following day in Belfast by the *Northern Whig*. Fisk notes in *In Time of War* that de Valera referred to the Luftwaffe raid as a 'disaster' as if it were a natural calamity rather than an act of war but a man with a famously meticulous mind and vocabulary chose the word deliberately. He could with a clear conscience and without fear of political or international complaint respond to a humanitarian disaster.

One of his primary concerns was the possible reaction of Germany to this patent example of aid to Britain. His relations with Hempel were rather less tense than they might have been. He had hoped without much expectation that the Luftwaffe would spare Northern Ireland, perhaps thinking that Hitler might morally extend Éire's resolute neutrality to include the 'occupied part' of Ireland. Nazi intelligence of the significant if not entirely industrious contribution of the Belfast workforce to the war effort could not be ignored by his high command. Hempel made no public comment but may have advised his superiors not to make any formal response. Redmond quotes a statement he made to the *Sunday Press* in an interview he gave in 1963. (He had been given political asylum by de Valera in 1945 when the Allies were bent upon rounding up any Nazi members still in Éire and he lived in Ireland for the rest of his life.) He said rather oddly: 'I think we could have protested. But it would have been cruel.' He also revealed that nobody from Germany protested and he had no desire to do so either.

There were no raids in Belfast after the last massive fire-bombing of early May 1941 but startlingly more Irish people would die in a Luftwaffe raid, this time on North Dublin. There had been several under-reported incidents already that year: on Wednesday, 1 January three bombs were dropped between Drogheda and Julianstown, four miles to the south in County Meath. Next day there was a further incursion by a German plane, dropping a bomb at Borris, County Carlow, and killing three people. The same night further attacks were made, with four bombs in Dublin, three in Wexford and three at the racecourse at the Curragh. (By sheer coincidence one of the buildings damaged was the Jewish synagogue in Adelaide Road but not everyone accepted it as pure mischance.) The Irish government decided to play down any significance they felt the raid might have. There was the usual suggestion by diehards that it was a propaganda move by the British to discredit Germany, to urge an end to neutrality and foster cooperation with the Allies. When the Drogheda bomb fragments proved to be German on forensic examination the three Dublin dailies reported that the Éire government had made 'strong protests' to Germany but none of them thought to write an editorial about the events. The one paper that did comment, as opposed to bland reportage, was censored by the highly efficient government office. Some suggested that Aiken's men were less interested in not mentioning the war than in controlling those who may have felt that Fianna Fáil was not the party of absolute probity. The heavily censored cinema newsreels (and Dublin had a right to claim to be in those years the movie-going capital of Europe) stated merely that the bombs had been dropped by an 'unidentified plane'. The phrase was repeated on Raidió Éireann, even though the papers, including the government-backed *Irish Press*, had declared the origin. The proof of origin did not convince the anti-British lobby who claimed that even if the bombs were made in Germany it was British planes that dropped them.

Even these innocent victims of extreme anti-British exaltation were silenced by the following June. Early on Saturday morning, 31 May, a few minutes after midnight, the local ARP wardens became aware of the presence of German planes. They too could identify them as Luftwaffe from the discontinuous sound of their engines and immediately set off flares to advise the pilots that they were over neutral territory, a fact that should have been obvious from the brightly lit towns over which they were flying. At 1.30am, a 250-pound bomb was dropped on North Circular Road, demolishing a house and killing all the occupants. Two bombs of similar poundage fell on Summerhill Parade, at the lower end of the North Circular, and in Phoenix Park, to the northwest, the latter causing no fatalities but damaging slightly Aras an Uachtaráin and the American embassy. At 2.05am, five hundred pounds of HE fell on the North Strand Road. All the missiles except for the one in the park fell within a quarter of a mile of each other. The last demolished twenty-five houses and rendered 345 unfit for use. The Dublin fire brigade rushed from Tara Street, little more than a mile away, and extinguished the fires in under the hour. Their Belfast brothers were quick to offer help. The *Independent* had time to print the story and was able to announce that the Belfast brigade offered to help, if required. There was no need but the gesture of solidarity was greatly appreciated and in 1942 there began a series of friendly soccer football matches.

Thirty-four people died, over half of them women and children, but the totals were not known for some weeks as more were gradually discovered during the clearing away of rubble. The raids caused a mixture of rage and horror but the prime emotion was that of bewilderment. William Warnock, the Irish government representative, immediately registered an official protest. Into the vacuum of speculation rushed all kinds of theories, mostly conspiratorial. Some suggested that the North Circular, that housed a number of Jewish families, was the target. (The same was said of the Antrim Road in Belfast for the same unlikely reasons.) Even more surreal was the lunatic fringe suggestion that German planes that had been captured were manned with British crews and that the raid was an attempt to make Ireland forsake her neutral stance. Forensic examination of bomb fragments established that they were of German origin. Some suggested that the Dublin bombs were in retaliation for Éire's help in Belfast and for the succour given to Belfast refugees. Others saw it as a dread warning of the consequences if cooperation with the Allies should increase. Hempel's own slightly desperate theory was that the system used by British anti-aircraft installations of distorting the radio beams the German planes used for navigation purposes had caused the raiding planes to believe that they were over a British city. The likeliest explanation was probably meteorological: a mist blown by winds off the Irish Sea may have covered the Dublin lights sufficiently to make the pilots believe that they had an appropriate target. One blackly comic memory of the time was that of a little girl, not yet nine, who recalls the queues for confession at St Peter's, Phibsborough, the nearest church to the scene of the bombing. It was mostly men who stood in the line that stretched from the door of the church right round the sharp corner on to the Cabra Road.

The post-war German government accepted responsibility for the raid and offered to pay compensation. The Ministry of Finance assessed the damage at £460,000 but it was not until 1958 that recompense of £327,000 was paid.

The story of the journey north lives as a bright interlude in Dublin–Belfast relations. The participants did not think of themselves as heroes. It was just another 'shout' and even among the firemen there were mixed emotions. Some believed that since Catholics were so obviously discriminated against in most aspects of their lives they might not expect equal treatment from the ARP and Belfast fire services. Most however knew that they were on their way to help fellow-countrymen and that is how most people reacted to the event. MacDermott's statement in Stormont on 22 April summed up the general feeling:

> The help afforded by our Southern neighbours was not related to any bond of war or to any political consideration. It was above and beyond politics; it was based on a common humanity and we gratefully acknowledge it as such.

The *Irish News*, then as now the voice of constitutional nationalism, managed in an editorial to temper sincerity with political nous:

> A word of high praise is due to the unstinted assistance given by our countrymen in the neutral part of this island to this area. Not only have they been prompt in sending their fire fighting units. No trouble is too great for the citizens of Eire when it is a question of housing and sheltering refugees. Never was sympathy so manifest; never pity so practised. We in our day of sorrow thank our countrymen from the South.

7

Ditching

THE SENSATION SEEKERS WHO TRAVELLED TO Belfast in the days after the Easter Week blitz had to come by train and bus; very few had cars and fewer still had petrol, only doctors, policemen, clergymen and those in other reserved occupations were granted an allowance. However most of the traffic then was away from the city, as people fled to safety. There were a number of main rail networks: the Great Northern Railway (GNR) travelled through Counties Antrim, Down (briefly), Armagh, Tyrone and Derry with its terminus at Foyle Road in the city. Offshoots went from Dungannon as far north as Cookstown and southwest though Armagh city and Monaghan to Clones and Cavan. The line's most important link was from Portadown Junction south through Dundalk and Drogheda to the terminus at Amiens Street in Dublin. This became the route of many mainly nationalist refugees from the city after the second raid. All the trains from the Wednesday morning on were met at the main stations by crowds offering them help in the way of food and cheer.

Among those who made their way to the crowded GNR station in Great Victoria Street were Paddy Carolan, his brother Eugene, two of his sisters and his stoical mother. Their father had managed to get in touch with his sister, Mary, who lived in a farmhouse at Tonyduff near Bailieborough in County Cavan. It was quite a feat, considering the general breakdown in communications. Even more amazing was his success in getting a taxi to call at the house in Marsden Gardens and negotiate the journey down the debris-filled Antrim Road to the station. At one stage, passing the top of the badly damaged Duncairn Gardens, the driver had to swing clear across to the right-hand side of the road and even then had to mount the pavement. The station was crowded with anxious people determined to get out of the once familiar but now dark and dangerous city. As many extra trains that could be marshalled were put into service, the ones coming from across the border fuelled mainly by peat. Eventually the Carolan family found seats in a Dublin train and travelled to Dundalk. They then made their way to Tonyduff by bus and hackney, where they stayed for four months. The children heard about the May blitz when their resourceful father sent a telegram to reassure the family that he and the three older sisters, Nancie, Kathleen Patricia and Marie, were safe. Nancie worked in a solicitor's office, Kathleen Patricia in Arnott's store that had been badly damaged.

Marie had been sent to keep her Aunt Minnie company in her house in Andersontown, then very much a rural suburb. During the height of the bombing early on the Wednesday morning of Easter Week, a crowd of mainly Catholics ditched in the Falls Park and, in an excess of piety and anxiety, lit candles. It was quite a sight and must have confused the observers in the Junkers and Heinkels wondering what kind of target could have produced such an odd display of lights. A friendly Presbyterian minister who lived next door to Aunt Minnie wondered at the wisdom of the display in the circumstances but, in fact, with the lights of the incendiary-generated fires and the bright-as-day flares, it made very little difference. The raids did call into question the whole business of the blackout but no one complained. The student teachers returned to the college on Monday, 21 April, but because of the uncertainty of the time those with homes in Belfast were allowed to live at home. In this way Marie spent the significant night of 4–5 May in her own house and survived.

When the Carolan family returned towards the end of August they were amazed at the scenes of destruction they witnessed. The day Paddy went back to school in Newington Avenue, there were less than twenty pupils in the whole building, from 'babies' to seventh class. As the fear of further raids decreased, marked by the entry of America into the war and the almost total cessation of the blitz in Britain, the school slowly recovered its normal population but the deeply ingrained fear kept many evacuees 'down the country', as the phrase went.

Another heroic story of the time that also ended safely in Cavan concerns the wife of a head constable in the RUC. When the Easter bombing was at its height, and with her husband off somewhere on duty, she calmly arranged her two boys and two girls in the small family car and drove all the way to her own family home in Cavan, even though she had never driven a car in her life before.

Those who could afford to travel and had contacts along the route in either Armagh or Down were ready to stay but the husbands of families could not live too far from the city and their workplace. Major O'Sullivan, the Éire military observer, reported:

> From the morning of the 16th and all throughout the day there was a continuous 'trek' to railway stations. The refugees looked dazed and horror-stricken and many had neglected to bring more than a few belongings – I saw one man with just an extra pair of socks stuck in his pocket. Any and every means of exit from the city was availed of and the final destination appeared to be a matter of indifference. At nightfall the Northern Counties station was packed from platform gates to entrance gates and still refugees were coming along in a steady stream from the surrounding streets... Open military lorries were finally put into service and even expectant mothers and mothers with young children were put into these in the heavy drizzle that lasted throughout the evening. On the 17th I heard that hundreds who either could not get away or could not leave for other reasons simply went out into the fields and remained in the open all night with whatever they could take in the way of covering.

The Northern Counties Committee (NCC) was the Ulster branch of the parent London, Midland and Scottish company with headquarters at Euston. It covered County Antrim and the north coast of Derry and its Belfast terminus at York Street had been damaged during the Holy Week raid. Looking at the present paucity of railways it is hard to believe that once the whole of Ireland was networked with track, a system that nowadays would be recognised as highly desirable and ecologically sound. Belfast had been a city really for only a few generations, and many of its inhabitants had country relations, grannies, uncles and aunts. The Protestant refugees would have headed mainly for Antrim and Down, using the NCC, the Bangor and County Down railways. Those were the lucky ones. It was recorded that the number of tickets sold at the York Road terminus during 1941 for Ballycarry, a County Antrim town five miles northeast of Carrickfergus, was six times the total for 1939. Many were not sure of their destinations and shocked, weary and afraid, could not even think beyond the coming night. Moya Woodhouse, a Belfast woman who was an important member of the team of Mass Observation, the project devised by Tom Harrisson (1911–76) to gather real information about the society of the day, kept a diary of the period. She was the wife of a Belfast surgeon and her records, preserved in the Mass Observation archive in Brighton, give a marvellously atmospheric picture of the city during the war. Her entries for 16 April 1941 and the following days paint a grim picture of the plight of the evacuees and the plight of their hosts:

> Evacuation is taking on panic proportions. Roads out of town are still one stream of cars, with mattresses and bedding tied on top. Everything on wheels is being pressed into service. People are leaving from all parts of town and not only from the bombed area. Where they are going, what they will find to eat when they get there, nobody knows. This business presents a problem of the first proportions to Stormont.

The significant sentence in the paragraph is the last. Even less focussed people than Mrs Woodside had realised that not only were there no systems of defence but that there were only the sketchiest of arrangements for the welfare of the citizens. True, no one expected the crisis and even those who knew raids were inevitable were appalled at the destruction, the huge number of casualties and the 100,000 refugees.

Even more appalling was the pitiful state of the poorer refugees. A city council dedicated to being kind to the ratepayers had made virtually no welfare arrangements for the poor. The 'public relief' riots a decade previously had been a clear warning, but that warning – like the warnings about the Luftwaffe's likely visits – had been, if actually received, shrugged off. The streams of families from working-class areas exhibited all the visible signs of neglect: malnutrition, physical debility and lack, even, of basic clothing but they could not show the terror and hopelessness underneath. Photographs of the time show children who could have acted as models for the pictures of Gustave Doré (1832–83) used by Lord Shaftesbury (1801–85) to illustrate the horrors of the factory system in the early days of the Industrial Revolution. Most of the volunteer hosts were middle-class country people or dwellers in smaller towns and they were incredulous and bewildered by the condition of the mothers and children whom they were asked to shelter. They were surprised by the realisation that most had rarely left their urban villages, much less the city, and they were appalled at their lack of toilet training. One WVS official, quoted in Brian Barton's book, stated that all the panic-stricken refugees needed to be 'fed, housed, deloused, marshalled, bathed, clothed, pacified and brought back to normal'.

The reaction of Emma Duffin, with its mixture of nausea, disbelief and yet some sympathy, was typical. She described 'the incredible dirt of the people, of children crawling with lice, not even house-trained, who destroyed mattresses and stuffed clothes down W.C.'s, in order to get new ones, women turning up with naked children who were fully dressed and the same women and the same children turning up at another rest centre the following day, the children once more naked'. The pawnbrokers were busy and Ms Duffin was becoming acquainted with the survival techniques of 'the submerged one-tenth of population'. She was also probably aware that a minority of unscrupulous property owners, equally adept at 'using the system' as the refugees, overcrowded their barns and bothies with as many people as they could cram in, heedless of the fact that there was not the semblance of proper hygienic arrangements. This lack, however, may not have greatly discommoded some of their clients.

Moya Woodhouse's mother took in eight evacuees – two mothers and six children. One of the mothers was imminently pregnant, all adults, as well as children, were filthy and 'the smell in the room is terrible. They refuse all food except bread and tea; the children have made puddles all over the floor etc.' A grandfather and two other children arrived making the total of her ingrate houseguests eleven. Out of her own resources she made them a tasty sausage pie – this at the height of food rationing– and a milk pudding. 'Both were sent back to the kitchen "messed about" but not eaten. "We don't like this sort of food." – "When are we going to have our tea?" – "We don't want that jam you gave us yesterday."' Moya's sister-in-law, an active WVS officer, living in a town thirty miles from Belfast, was stunned by

> … the appalling influx from the slums the day after the raid… The whole town is horrified by the filth of these evacuees and by their filthy habits and their take-it-for-granted attitude… The smell is awful… They don't even use the lavatory, they just do it on the floor, grown-ups and children, our blankets in two nights have been absolutely ruined.

She was mortified as a WVS welfare officer to have to ask 'decent working people to take in such guests'. She was also aware that many had TB and skin complaints. The greater shock to such right-minded people was not the condition of individual refugee families but of the universal misery of so many people who lived all the time where such conditions were the norm.

The irascible Dawson Bates, the incompetent Minister of Home Affairs, earned himself a permanent footnote in any future history of Northern Ireland with his comment:

> There is unfortunately a class that can only be described as unbilletable
> and which the Ministry would be very loath to billet on any householder
> in Northern Ireland, such people are so inhuman in their habits.

He and MacDermott (with, one would suspect, some reluctance on the latter's part) wrote a joint memorandum for the already dysfunctional cabinet that 'Lice and vermin are being spread through the country, buses and trains are being infected, and clean and well-kept households are having billeted upon them filthy and verminous persons.' Even more striking than the insensitive and uncaring tone of the memorandum was the complete derogation of any responsibility for the conditions that were being described.

To be fair the scale of the exodus was hugely beyond all expectations. Many of the estimated 100,000 refugees had come from undamaged houses and had taken over the refuges intended for the genuinely homeless. They would have argued that they could well be the next to be targeted in the inevitable coming attack of the Luftwaffe. All the official agencies were utterly swamped and any amelioration of distress came about through heroic individual efforts. There was no communication between the ARP and the RUC. Reception areas had to shut their doors because they could not accommodate any more clients. Even a properly organised welfare system, such as existed in the larger English cities, could not have coped with the surge of what MacDermott called 'blitz-quitters', including trained members of the ARP. He had to admit that no other United Kingdom city had so many of these 'quitters'. As Sam Hanna Bell had noted in his memoir in the *Honest Ulsterman*, some of the Civil Defence personnel led the exodus. One warden was spotted still wearing his regulation overalls and carrying his helmet marked ARP on the platform in Amiens Street Station, the Dublin terminus of the GNR. Others, however, stayed and like the nurses, ambulance drivers, bobbies on the beat, members of the WVS and other welfare services and even individual members of the public, who, forgetting self-interest, answered a Samaritan call.

It was in Dickensian terms 'the best of times and the worst of times'. The sponging of the 'submerged tenth' and their exploiting of the limited welfare resources was at least understandable. It was a part of their survival instinct and though not statistically aware of it they knew that their children were more prone to long-drawn-out illnesses, undernourishment, weak physique and shorter life expectancy. The exploitative rack-renters of shanty shelters to desperate refugees from terror was less excusable. Their cashing-in on the misfortunes of others could have been technically defended as providing a service that the authorities themselves did not seem capable of providing but it had become a racket notably at variance with the true spirit of the war effort. The charge was also made that some of the recipients exploited the children under their care, treating them as hired hands and overloading them with farmyard chores, of which they had no experience. In contrast some billet-owners treated their charges with care and kindliness, educating slum children to a much richer and fuller life and establishing friendships that were to last long after the war was over. For those who could afford alternative accommodation in the country it was in a sense a return to roots, and country cousins were regarded with much greater respect from then on.

John Blake describes in his history the evolution of an improvised unofficial welfare centre. A church hall in the southern suburbs was selected as a centre on the morning of 16 April 1941 but was given no resources. Once nominated it was crowded each evening for the next dozen weeks. Some clients were essential workers who were required to report each day and could not afford to be billeted outside of the city. Others were genuinely homeless and had literally no shelter. Still others had perfectly sound dwellings but were understandably scared of the effects of another raid. And the rest had hated their assigned provincial billets and had instinctively burrowed their way back to the warm city. The hall had been assigned no equipment and because of the lack of a gas supply, due to fractured mains, there was no means of heating or cooking. Volunteers, both WVS members and local housewives, brought pots and pans from their own kitchens. The centre supervisor was able to borrow the delf from the church and a woman brought a spirit stove. Some blankets arrived from a government store and local ARP officers searched the city for food for the guests. Members of the Home Guard (mainly recruited from the Ulster B-Special Constabulary) helped supervise the refugees. A battery of doctors and nurses, all volunteers, made the necessary preliminary medical examinations. In time, when the emergency slowly receded, the Ministry of Home Affairs, outwardly unmoved but secretly chastened, organised that centre and other similar ad hoc venues on a proper basis. Much has been made in British folklore of the spirit of the Blitz among cheery Cockneys saying 'Wotcher, mate!', ignoring the actual terror, the black-market dealings, the minor criminal rackets and the genuine fear of proletarian revolution. Here not enough tribute has been paid to the instinctive generosity of Belfast people towards the afflicted in dire need in the worst weeks of their war.

There were two recognisable characteristics of the Belfast citizens who were determined to avoid death in a future air raid: fear and an even greater instinct for survival. The government could not cope with the flood of people leaving the city by any means of transport: train, car, bus, lorry, bicycle and many on foot. They had plans for the care of at most a notional 10,000 but ten times that number were clamouring for attention on that Wednesday. The smaller towns near the city – Lisburn, Moira, Lurgan, Dromore, Ballynahinch, Downpatrick – found that their populations increased, literally overnight. Lina Purdie, a teacher in Crossgar, County Down, remembered that 'one day I had fourteen children and the next day I had forty-eight… They walked out of Belfast… into Crossgar and just took over.' Most had walked and bivouacked the sixteen miles and the invasion of Miss Purdie's classroom had more to do with seeking shelter and provisions than education. Bates reported to the cabinet that the County Down village of Dromara, four miles south of Hillsborough and sixteen miles from the city as the refugee scuttles, which had a native population of 500, had received 1,500 extra bodies by the end of April. This was typical of many villages within a radius of forty miles from Belfast and food supplies were running dangerously low. Sir Basil Brooke, who, as an efficient Minister of Agriculture, had grave concerns about the spread of infectious disease, was very upset when refugees made their way as far west as his own county of Fermanagh.

Health considerations were even more vital for the nightly 'ditchers'. A number of citizens who retained some semblance of habitation decided that the city was no longer a place fit to spend the night in. Though as many as 100,000 claimed to have been made homeless some still had undamaged dwellings. Even the figure given represented less than a quarter of the population and most ditchers returned to their homes at dawn, quite late with Double British Summer Time (DBST) advancing the clocks by two hours, or earlier if they sensed that there was less danger or that the peril had passed. There was no point in the truly homeless ditching since they had top priority for relocation. There was a kind of urban resistance to the country. Most, as someone said, had never been beyond the tram terminuses and their attitude to culchies was rather that of Dublin jackeens who believed that the bogs (and bogmen) began at Tallaght. The origin of the term 'ditching' was a characteristically unfeeling and injudicious remark of Craigavon in the last year of his life at a cabinet meeting in 1940. At a conference about the protection of Belfast people in case of aerial attack he brushed MacDermott's concerns aside, saying, 'The country is near and they can take to the ditches.' In extenuation one can say that he was prone to such bluff, 'no-nonsense' remarks, that he was less mentally acute because of illness ('ga-ga' according to Lady Londonderry) and it never occurred to him that the risk of bombing was real.

Fear and reluctance to face the unknown kept many people in a kind of halfway state, going about their business and apparently normal by day and understandably hag-ridden when darkness fell, especially on nights naturally lit by moon and stars. Herbert Morrison, Churchill's Home Secretary from 1940, though they detested each other, sent Andrews a telegram early on the Thursday morning. It was a gesture and little more:

> Whilst grieved to hear of the air raid on Northern Ireland last night and sending sincere sympathy to bereaved and injured I warmly congratulate leaders and people on their grit and courage. As arranged with you two officers leaving here for Northern Ireland tomorrow. All help we can send is at your disposal.

The last sentence is a fine example of a politician's weasel words but his praise of 'grit and courage' rings a little bit hollow. With a few exceptions the leaders showed neither virtue, and a majority showed little else than attempts at salutary self-protection. There was a contemporary joke about the response of an able-bodied refugee when asked if he had no concern for king and country. His reply echoed in the heads of many similarly inclined: 'To hell with the king; I'm for the country!' There *were* many deeds of outstanding heroism: three George Medals (the highest civilian award for valour) and six British Empire Medals were awarded but there were few heroes, nor was there any reason why there should have been.

Some patterns of behaviour are so deeply ingrained as to be almost instinctual. Even 'ditching' was for some ideological as well as topographical. The convenience of green sites to all parts of Belfast meant that most ditchers drifted radially in a city that already presented something of the model and even the rough appearance of a dartboard. Immediately outside the commercial centre was a roughly circular band of lower working-class dwellings associated with the yards, mills and factories where the denizens found employment. Another concentric band held the houses of skilled artisans, with a further band holding the suburban houses of those in the professions: teachers, academics, doctors, lawyers. A further intermittently broken circuit contained the dwellings of the lordly ones: the rich, the community leaders whose villas were often decently obscured by mounting greenery. To complete the dartboard analogy the radial roads that delimited the sectors also acted rather like notional borders between self-contained communities. Counter-clockwise from the north there was a series of arteries: Shore, Antrim, Cliftonville, Crumlin, Shankill, Grosvenor/Springfield, Falls, Donegall/Whiterock, Lisburn, Malone, Ormeau/Ravenhill, Cregagh, Castlereagh, Newtownards and Holywood almost completing the circle on the east side of the lough. There was in general intensive building between pairs of radials, with the exception of the Bog Meadows between the Falls and Lisburn, and the middle-class suburbs to the south between Lisburn and Ormeau.

Ditchers were by definition part of the perceived 'submerged tenth' that had neither the means nor the organisational abilities to seek more permanent shelter. They were also instinctively rooted to their home districts. Police reports indicated that two miles was the greatest distance that most of them travelled for safety. Around the city, again counter-clockwise from shore to shore, were suitable places for ditching under the shelter of Belfast's lowering hills: Carnmoney, Squires Hill, Wolf Hill, Divis, Black Mountain and Collin. The green areas immediately under these sentinels were popular picnic places. Cave Hill and Hazelwood had long been Belfast's largest urban park and it was the most natural thing in the world for overnight refugees from the beleaguered Shore Road and Antrim Road to find their ditches there, though some preferred Greencastle. The ditchers of Cavehill Road, Old Park Road and Cliftonville Road preferred the Carr's Glen end of what has since become known as Cave Hill Country Park. The people from the Shankill had the small Woodvale Park at the top of the road and the land between the foothills of the Black Mountain and the boundary of patterned housing.

Anticipating the later hospitality of the Redemptorist priests and brothers when, during the May raids, the deep cellars of Clonard monastery were made available as shelters to any women and children who came seeking safety, a number of Shankill people joined Catholics ditching in the grounds there to share again their common adversity with citizens of the Lower Falls and Divis Street. Falls Park, Colin Glen and Hannahstown provided shelter for the rest of the Falls and the Upper Springfield, though the lower part of the latter was avoided because it contained Mackie's foundry that was known to be deeply involved in munitions manufacture. For the same reason, the Holywood Road, with the Shorts factory so close, was avoided. This awareness of likely targets was at variance with the previous surprise 'that anyone would want to bomb Belfast'.

Lisburn Road people who wished to ditch had the Bog Meadows, now a nature reserve and once a kind of buffer zone between them and the Catholic Falls. The people of east Belfast had Dundonald, and the gentler hills of Castlereagh and Cregagh. Relying on age-own instincts they made shelters for themselves in parks, fields, under hedgerows, until the spring dawn, returning then to their homes. The lucky ones found sheds, abandoned barns, crude shelters under trees. Some were allowed by accommodating farmers to bed down in hay-sheds, empty and ready for the June harvest. Some found refuge even in the large pipes that drained the hills. There was on the whole, though with some exceptions, an agreement about admittedly temporary 'ownership'. Individual families brought bedding, rainwear, vacuum flasks and the holy pictures, up-beat tasks gradually improving the amenities of the nests that gave them shelter. Some authorities suggested a total of 10,000 people who were believed to be ditching on a nightly basis but others suggested that this figure was a serious underestimation.

The greatest concentration of ditching occurred in the months mid-April to mid-August with a surge of numbers after the May fire-raids. The twilight roads were customarily thronged with the mobile night travellers. They were fortunate in the time of year and in the lack of night frosts, with a steadily decreasing number of hours of darkness. The weather stayed warm and the dreaded epidemic of typhoid was avoided. It was a mercy that the raids were not the prelude to invasion and the dropping of paratroops because the crowded roads and the deserted city would have combined to make the total *Blitzkrieg* very short and sharp indeed. Barbarossa saved Belfast's skin and also Derry's, and prevented the nightmare of a partially occupied Ulster and a kind of Vichy regime in Éire. One of the government's sharpest critics in every aspect of its rule, except its stance on the political integrity of the Northern Ireland state, was the independent Unionist, Tommy Henderson (1877–1970). In a blistering attack on Andrews and his handling of civilian security, he summed up the plight of the ditchers:

> Will he come to the hills and to the Divis Mountain? Will he go to the barns and the sheughs throughout Northern Ireland to see the people of Belfast, some of them lying on damp ground?… Will he come to Hannahstown and the Falls Road? The Catholics and the Protestants are going up there mixed and they are talking to one another. They are sleeping in the same sheughs, below the same trees and in the same barns. They all say the same thing, that the Government is no good.

The government had a lot to answer for and there were more horrors, suffering and even greater recriminations to come.

The city amenity systems had taken a beating. Loss of power because of attacks on generating stations, and fractured water mains and sewers raised the spectre of disease. Advertisements and news stories appeared in the Belfast papers warning against typhoid. On Monday, 28 April, the *Northern Whig* printed a recommendation from the city medical officer that all drinking water should be boiled and advised that those who had survived in badly bombed areas should present themselves for inoculation. A week earlier the *Belfast News Letter* had reported that, of fifty-seven deaths from infectious diseases that week, two had died of typhoid. Tuberculosis was also a killing disease then and nights in the ditches, even in mild weather, was the last thing an MO would countenance. Yet so demoralised were the ditchers, and so distrustful of the authorities, that for the whole summer and the early autumn of 1941 the foothills of the city were crowded with unwilling bivouackers. As the summer wore on and no further raids occurred the numbers of ditchers began to decrease but any sound of a siren had them bundling back again to their alternative, emergency accommodation.

8

Derry's Own Blitz

THE MAIN BUSINESS OF EASTER WEEK in Derry was, and is, Féis Doire Colmcille. The festival of Irish singing, dancing and speech was nineteen years old that April and the Guildhall was full of the sound of soloists, choirs and the tattoo of taps on wooden boards. The war had of course impinged on the second city of Ulster but in the Great Hall and the Minor Hall there was hardly a thought of danger. If Belfast people had believed that the city would not be bombed Derry people knew for certain that the oak grove of Colum Cille was invulnerable. Who would want to bomb us? Didn't the saint promise that no disaster would ever afflict his beloved city?

The highlight of the evening session on the Tuesday was the Junior Action Song, a kind of dramatic cantata sung entirely in Irish. The Great Hall was always crowded to the rafters with parents and children, enough to make one of today's Elfan Safetee officers faint dead away. Most of the children had been taken home by 10.30 but there were still many people in the building enjoying the later competitions. The sirens sounded at 10.40 and the platform steward announced that a raid was imminent. No one in the audience showed any sign of alarm – they knew from experience that the sighting of German planes over the Irish Sea was responded to with a general alert – but parents who still had young children with them in the auditorium hurried them home. When they became conscious of unusual noise of ack-ack and the landmines, many bundled them under the stairs, as again 'the safest place in the house'. As CEM Joad (1891–1953), the star of *The Brains Trust*, a popular radio programme of the time, was fond of saying, 'It all depends on what you mean by safe.' For scores of people who lived in gerrybuilt houses it was anything but safe.

Charlie Gallagher was on ARP duty that night and he recalls in his book, *Acorns and Oak Leaves* (1981), that when the alert began he went to his first-aid post at the corner of Queen Street and Great James Street close to the Guildhall. All was quiet for more than an hour until the word came through that, 'Belfast was being hammered again.' One of the voluntary first-aid officers asked the company to join her in prayer 'for those who may die tonight'. Not long afterwards one of the wardens looked outside his post and discovered that flares were being dropped. Then came two 'deafening explosions' and an emergency call for numbers one and two ambulances to be sent to an 'incident' at Messines Park. Gallagher was driver of number two and he remembers that his Talbot 'started on the button' and went haring round the corner of Great James Street and Strand Road. It was a beautiful moonlit night with broken cloud, perfect for the Luftwaffe's purpose, and he reached the corner of Buncrana Road in less than five minutes. As the ambulance turned the corner normal sounds seemed different. There seemed to be fog and from the strange note of the tyres he felt he was driving over earth, as though he were in a field. The fog he realised was dust borne on thermals and the odd sound the tyres made was due to the sand that had covered the tarmac. An ARP warden loomed up out of the artificial haar: 'Corner of Messines Park. Direct hit on two houses. There's a naval rescue team; that's their floodlights. Stand by for their instructions.'

It became clear that two landmines had been dropped, perhaps intended for the narrow opening of Ross's Bay where the River Foyle empties into the lough. This would have effectively blocked the exit for the many warships at anchor in the city. One mine floated down behind Collon Terrace and landed innocuously in a sandpit sending up the dust storm that had seemed like mist in the headlights of Gallagher's ambulance. Later piety claimed that the statue of St Patrick, in its niche high in the offset tower, topped by the striking onion-shaped dome of St Patrick's Church, Pennyburn, had directed it manually away from the building. At the heavenly inquiry his colleague St Colum Cille was exonerated from dereliction of duty in keeping his promise to obviate any disaster in Derry since the mine that did the damage had fallen outside the city boundary. Faith can move more than mountains.

By one of those ironies beloved of shanachies the site of the destruction, Messines Park, had originally been named after a fierce battle of the Great War, fought at Messines Ridge near Ypres in Belgium in June 1917. The houses were built for veterans of the war in a neat layout with uniform design and gardens back and front. Some have suggested that the orderliness of the design may have made the residential park look like a military installation. From the air it might have been mistaken for a minuscule version of Ebrington Barracks, on the east bank of the Foyle, which had been a military garrison since 1837. As HMS *Sea Eagle* it played an important part in plotting aircraft positions and would undoubtedly have been known to German Intelligence.

Parachute landmines depended on gravity but were susceptible to crosswinds and were rigged to explode before they reached ground level. Richard Doherty, Derry's leading military historian, believes that the target was the naval yard at Pennyburn, which included a large graving dock used to repair the damaged destroyers and corvettes of the North Atlantic run. He opines that a high wind blew them in a north-northwest direction away from their intended target. Another theory advanced was that they were intended as magnetic mines that, attaching themselves to any of the many ships that used the channel, would not only have sunk the vessel but blocked the narrow outlet.

It is thought that the pilot dropped two of the 1,500lb mines into the river and that they sank to the muddy bottom of the tidal river without exploding but there is no record of their ever having been activated by contact by any of the ships that continued to use Derry as the chief centre for Western Approaches until the end of the war in 1945. In 1943, its peak year, it sheltered up to 150 vessels. Lisahally, the place where the mining was to take place, was the scene of the surrender in 1945 of forty U-Boats, the clearest sign that the war, in Europe, at least, was over.

If such was the mission of that single bomber it failed because two of the mines were blown off course to the southwest and caused Derry's only civilian casualties. At the time most people believed that the pilot had somehow become detached from the formation intent on obliterating the docks in Belfast. It does seem unlikely that a single aircraft would have been sent on a planned mission. There is no record among German archives of any formal intention to bomb Derry. Twenty minutes of flight time could have brought a stray bomber over Lough Foyle that could have been mistaken for Belfast Lough on a cloudy night. The pilot, finding himself on his own and with a lethal load that would have been unsafe to carry home, may have jettisoned it as soon as he got his bearings over the now moonlit Lough Foyle. Relieved of his deadly cargo he flew towards Inishowen Head, rounded Malin Head, the most northerly point on the Irish mainland, and followed the west Irish coast right to Cape Clear and then back to his home field in France. Once in Éire airspace he was unlikely to have been fired on. The actual nature of the mission, if it can be dignified with that description, is still a matter of heated debate, especially among Derry people who remember that fateful night. The balance of the argument is strongly on the side of 'shurely shome mishtake', in the deathless words of Bill Deedes.

Gallagher's ambulance had had to stop short of Messines Park because the mine explosion had caused a deep crater now filling with water from mains and sewers. Underground telephone cables were exposed and the expert naval rescue team, equipped with mobile floodlights, were already sifting through the rubble. When one large piece of rubble was cleared – part of the wall of a house – it revealed the body of a woman in bed, apparently without a scratch, but dead of shock or blast. There was a book beside her on the pillow. In all, thirteen bodies were identified that night or the next day. Fifty-five Messines Park had been the home of the Collins family and the mine blew down the gable wall. James Collins, who had been born in 1880 and had served in the Royal Navy in the Great War, and his twenty-one–year-old daughter Ellen died when the wall fell; they were buried at Glendermot New Cemetery. Next door in number 57 William Alexander McFarland, a member of the Home Guard, died but his wife Elizabeth had spent the night in her parents' house in Hawkin Street and it was there that the body was waked before burial in the City Cemetery. The Murray family, next door at number 59, had consisted of parents William (50) and Mollie (39), and children Kathleen (by a previous marriage), Ita (13), Philomena (10), and Sheila (10 months), who all died together. Sixty-one Messines Park had been the home of the Richmonds: father John (53), mother Winifred (45), their son Owen (18), and baby daughter Bridie (14 months).

Another unidentified body was later discovered under rubble removed from the bomb site during road building by American 'technicians', as an army of civilian construction engineers were called by locals when they came to build tactical buildings. Such constructions as the submarine school were said to be part of Roosevelt's 'innocent' Lend-Lease agreement with Churchill but were clearly anti-German and increased Derry's likelihood as a target. The Derry papers were still bound by stern censorship regulations and could not specify the location of the destruction. The *Londonderry Sentinel* of 17 April told of 'a raid on a Northern Ireland town' when a number of people were killed and injured and of how a 'Union Jack floated bravely over the pile of debris, which is practically all that remains of four houses, two semi-detached dwellings, in an ex-service men's colony on the outskirts of the town'. The picture of devastation, of rubble tangled with the domestic furniture of the so recently alive, summed up the shocking misery of a war against civilians:

> At the bottom of a crater, from which the water was still being pumped, lay a soaked armchair. Near the edge of the crater, lying on the heap of rubble, was the couch of the suite. Embedded in the side of the crater beneath was the wreckage of a piano. Mixed up in the midst of the pile were all kinds of furniture, some of which escaped damage.

The same report mentioned the Roman Catholic Church and Parochial House that lost many windows. The priest-in-charge, Patrick O'Loughlin (1894–1969), ministered to the victims but was seriously affected by what is now known as post-traumatic stress and never quite recovered from the experience. He was soon transferred to Omagh and preferred to remain a curate for the rest of his ministry. A ex-naval man called Brown, also from Messines Park, seeing the flares and hearing the noise of the ack-ack, bundled his six children into one large bed, told them to pull the bedclothes over their heads and pushed it between the two bedroom windows. They all escaped injury, as did he, crouching in a back room. As soon as he reassured his children that the danger was past he ran to the demolished houses and began to assist at rescue. He heard a baby crying under the rubble and dug the child out from between two dead parents. The woman hailed as the heroine of the 'minor blitz', according to the *Sentinel*, was the eighty-year-old Mrs Gilfillan, who had refused to leave her bed even after the windows and door had been blown in and her bed showered with plaster.

The *Derry Journal* did not publish the story until its edition of Friday, 18 April. The Wednesday edition had been put to bed before the raid and its headline was the unspecific: 'Raid on Six County Town'. It never quite accepted partition and used Ulster only in its historical nine-county context. Its three subheads appropriately summed up the night's events: 'Ex-Servicemen's Houses Destroyed; People Killed and Injured; Remarkable escapes.' The main text kept well on the windy side of the censor. The second mine, which landed in a sandpit, shattered the windows and removed the roof tiles of the church and presbytery, and those of the houses, not only of immediately neighbouring streets, Maybrook Terrace, St Patrick's Terrace, St Brigid's Avenue, Collon Terrace and New Street, but some as relatively far away as Balmoral Avenue. The site of the explosion of this mine was described rather misleadingly as 'in open country'. True, there were houses on only one side but it was really still in the town and not, as the *Journal* suggested, truly rural. In one case the front door of a house was blown through the back door. A Mr Collins, who had a public house-cum-grocery on the side of the Buncrana Road, away from the demolished houses, described how he was blown across the floor and, as the roof lifted, a large quantity of the pub's stock was blown out on to the road.

By the time this edition of the paper was published the absolute shock had diminished a little, at least during the hours of daylight, and the conversation had turned to consider the stories of survival. A boy aged twelve was blown out of bed but was uninjured in spite of flying glass and rubble blown into his house. Another boy, named as Daniel Diggin (14), though buried under a heap of plaster and rubble but protected by a pile of heavy framed pictures, was pulled out from the rubble without a scratch. Stephen Rabbitt, the owner of a small shop, had been outside when he saw the parachute bomb float gently down. He ran into the kitchen of his house where his mother and father were sitting. They all escaped injury but his shop and house furniture were destroyed. There was a swift response, both official and voluntary, to aid the survivors, many of whom had no place to live because of damage to their homes.

The *Derry Standard* took quite a gung-ho attitude to the raid, certainly compared with the *Journal*, which had to balance its horror at the event with its political stance of not being terribly pro-British.

The *Standard*'s headline on page five of the edition of Friday, 18 April, read: 'These People Have Courage' followed by the subhead: 'German Bombs Strengthened Their Morale.' It was typical of too exacting a kowtow to the censor that the only mark of location was the phrase 'in a bombed district visited by a special correspondent of the *Standard*'. This correspondent's selection of the scattered pathetic debris of the explosions was different from that of other papers: 'a child's toy tin helmet, a battered tennis racquet, the National Identity card of a victim' but it carried the evidence that 300 people were evacuated from the area. About half were able to make private arrangements with friends or find alternative accommodation. The rest were found shelter in officially commandeered houses outside the town. Tribute was paid to the local WVS who 'did noble work in providing transport, seeing to clothing...'It is worthwhile noting here that many of the workers who did their best to alleviate the sufferings of bomb victims were volunteers. Many of them were nationalists and their volunteering was an example of quiet heroism. Not all approved of helping with the war effort. Opposition ranged on a scale from 'It's England's war, not ours' to the old war-cry 'England's difficulty; Ireland's opportunity!' In fact, most of those, from the young to the able-bodied retired, worked 'not for flag or king or emperor' but out of kindness and an awareness of general suffering. The *Standard*'s coverage concluded with three short but telling sentences: 'The last body was taken from the rubble late yesterday afternoon. The number of fatal casualties is not yet definitely known. The funerals of a number of the victims will take place today.'

A standard government notice, containing 'ten simple facts' that should be known if the city be bombed again, was reissued. It stated starkly: 'Air raids may come again any night. You may lose your home.' The ten points covered 'Rest Centres' that would open after the 'Raiders Passed' signal. Food and shelter would be available and homeless victims could register there for emergency billeting. The second point dealt with homelessness certificates, which could be obtained from the nearest ARP post, the location of which, like the nearest rest centres, should have been already determined. The certificate was your ticket for billeting in or near the city if you were a worker, or evacuation if you were in a priority class. It was also the means of obtaining financial help, offered in point four most quickly. The third advised a visit as soon a possible after the All Clear to the District Information Bureau (DIB) where advice could be given to the stricken. Financial help was available and victims were advised to claim for war damage compensation, the DIB form to be completed within three days of the raid. Bureaucracy is absolutely necessary in most social situations but one always gets the impression that these regulations were more for the convenience of the officials rather than the needs of the afflicted.

The DIB had forms for furniture replacement, and for enquiries about the condition of friends. The priority class were defined in point eight: 'children, expectant mothers, mothers accompanying children, women accompanying infirm persons to look after them, persons incapable of working by reason of age or infirmity and blind persons. All others are regarded as workers and will be billeted in or near the city.' Work must go on; we want no slackers! Point nine offered meals in Emergency Feeding Centres 'at moderate prices'. Number ten urged people to look after themselves with its message in bold type:

> Arrange your own city billets. You have a house. Your friends have a house. You may lose yours but they will put you up for a time.

The rather stern tone was mitigated a little with the promise that 'the Government will pay a temporary billeting allowance'.

In spite of the raid the Féis continued its run that week, ending with the special parade of talent, the Prizewinners' Concert, on the Saturday evening. With an admirable if perhaps unwise defiance, féis-goers filled the Guildhall each night. This was less foolhardy than it may seem. Already those who could afford it had arranged for night accommodation across the border in Donegal, only a few miles from the city, in Carrigans, St Johnston, Fahan, Moville and Buncrana. Soon many Derry people rented houses in these places and at an appropriate time of day, after work, left the city for the safety of the neutral country. The GNR Belfast train, christened by one of the night-time refugees the 'Yellow Express', took them the four miles to Carrigans or the further two to St Johnston. A majority went to Buncrana and the last Londonderry and Lough Swilly train to run each evening was known as the 'Blitz Train'. A large majority, of course, could not afford the luxury of a cross-border pied-à-terre. For some weeks, as spring gave way to summer, a number of Derry people trekked each evening to the safer hills on both banks of the Foyle. There in makeshift sleeping bags on Corrody, Braehead, Holywell Hill and Sheriff's Mountain, they did the Derry equivalent of 'ditching'.

One veteran of the Messines Park blitz was Bertie Downey, who, then thirty-one years of age, had a house and shoemaking business less than fifty yards from where the one of the landmines made its stately descent. He recorded his memories for local radio in his ninety-first year in April 2001, the sixtieth anniversary of the raid. His house was one of many damaged by the blast that was the particular product of the parachute mines. He found it sadly ironic that four of the dead had survived the Great War only to die in their beds less than a quarter of a century later. He recalled the trepidation he felt as he waited outside the room in the City and County Hospital where the dead were laid out. He had been asked by the police to help identify the bodies of what had been near neighbours and he felt a mixture of dread and relief that he had survived. He was one of the earliest country refugees, heading out to his brother's house a few miles away at Galliagh. He remembered that the Buncrana Road was black with people that April morning as all those who lived near where the paramines had landed sought shelter in Donegal. He was asked by the interviewer how Derry Catholics felt about the Germans then.

He laughed and said that whatever about being pro-German they were certainly anti-British, though less so after Derry's blitz. He recalled with a chuckle that, as in Dublin six weeks later, the queues for confession were striking in size and fervour.

The terror persisted and, as in Belfast, the sound of a siren would send Derry people scurrying out of danger. Many others, less well organised, more phlegmatic or bloody-minded, stayed at home using the tested 'under the stairs' as the safest place in a raid. Some houses were equipped with Morrison shelters, if one of the dwellers were ill or infirm, and the whole family sought shelter in the large steel cage set up in their parlours. The realisation that Derry was a prime target and well within range of the captured airfields in northwest France changed people's perception of their security. Yet Derry, a severely depressed town in the 1920s and 1930s, had become a much livelier place. The coming of the 'Yanks', as they were imprecisely dubbed – many of them came from Texas and other southern states – left the city awash with Lucky Strike, Philip Morris and Camel cigarettes, and Hershey and Baby Ruth chocolate bars – this in a city blighted with sweet rationing. The first wave of these free spending, generous aliens were civilian construction experts, anticipating America's entering the war. They arrived in June 1941, nearly six months before Pearl Harbor. They built camps filled with Quonset huts at Springtown, Creevagh and Clooney that would house the US Marine Corps and other service personnel. Each was complete with a PX (from the words 'post exchange'), an Aladdin's cave, as they seemed to the deprived local employees, filled with unimaginable goodies. The camp theatre at Springtown hosted such megastars as Al Jolson and Bob Hope, sent to lift the hearts of the GIs so far from home and facing a grim future. They also constructed an anti-submarine training school and greatly improved the telecommunications of the region.

America entered the war immediately after the Japanese attack on the US fleet at anchor in Pearl Harbor in Hawaii on 7 December

1941. Next day Germany and Italy responded by declaring war on America and the whole tenor of the struggle changed. Six weeks later, on 26 January 1942, Private 1st Class Milburn H Henke, from Hutchinson, Minnesota, the first 'doughboy' to land on Irish soil, stepped on to Dufferin Quay in Belfast. American soldiers had been called 'doughboys' since 1848, but the term 'GI' (government issue), stamped on all their equipment and uniforms, led them to apply this name ironically to themselves, and its use was general by 1943.

America, just about recovered from the Great Depression following the Wall Street Crash of 1929, had almost unlimited resources of men and materials. The Construction Battalions (CBs) no longer had to pretend to be civilian but taking as a title the sound of their initials became the 'Fighting Seabees'. The effect on Derry was remarkable. Its provincial streets were filled with US forces, marines and doughboys, en route for North Africa, Sicily and Italy, and in 1943–44, preparing for D-Day. The 'regulars', however, were sailors on the turnover leave from the North Atlantic destroyers and corvettes. Their hazardous task was to protect the convoys of merchant ships bringing essential supplies across the U-Boat filled Atlantic. Their cargoes included concentrated orange juice and cod liver oil, rich sources of Vitamin C and D, that were made available free for children. (One commonly held belief was that they were diverted in some families away from the children and given to greyhounds.) The sailors had five days' leave while their vessels were refitted and they spent money as if there would literally be no tomorrows.

The war generally and the presence of the Yanks in particular provided Derry with near full employment for men, a condition unknown since the founding of the Northern Ireland state cut off the city's hinterland of Donegal and Sligo. Many Derrymen got jobs for the first time in their adult lives. The independent Derry women, safely employed in the shirt industry, were instinctively positive and friendly to the newcomers. This Irish hospitality was often misinterpreted by the boys in blue on short-time shore leave but a few sharp reminders cleared up any misconceptions the fleet may have had. To those who were disappointed that they did not wear the same neat little white caps as featured by Fred Astaire in *Follow the Fleet* (1936), they replied that Derry was the only port where they had to wear winter uniform. They could not help but be appalled at the amount of rain that fell. One Seabee was heard to say that the barrage balloons were there to keep 'this goddam place from sinking' and another observed that for half of the year Lough Foyle is in County Derry and for the other six months County Derry is in Lough Foyle. The town eventually made its quota of GI brides and when the 'Yanks' left in 1945, they were sorely missed. Derry also had its share of Free French, Free Dutch, Royal Canadian Navy servicemen, and occasional visits from Russians who had little money but frequently complained, 'In Russia, Stalin, he pay for all.'

It must have occurred to any thinking citizen that since the technicians, easily identifiable from their exotic, left-hand-drive vehicles – Buick, Chevrolet, Ford Sedans and Jeep – were busy in actually building a naval base on the Foyle, the city was becoming increasingly a prime target of further visits from the Luftwaffe. The tonnage of ships that used the base was more than one million for each of the years 1941–44 and reached its highest in 1943 with a record 1,700,873.

Derry, and Ulster as a whole, was saved by Hitler's ambition to succeed where Napoleon had failed. His decision to invade Russia in June 1941 changed the balance of the war in Europe, and America's entry that December spelled the end of the Axis ability to win it. With America, Britain, the USSR, Canada, Australia, New Zealand and Canada ranged against them the Axis were already defeated, though many lives were to be lost in the next four years. Derry was not attacked again, though on the night of the 4–5 May, when Belfast was incinerated by an incendiary firestorm, a bomb fell in the middle of a flock of sheep at Malin in County Donegal, about twenty-five miles from the city.

The remaining years of the war meant excitement without danger for a small city that had known little of comfort or glamour or decent employment. By 1944 the dim-out had replaced the blackout and the church bells, silent for so long, since they were to be the signal of a German invasion, were heard again. With the historian's great gift of hindsight we can understand that Derry's avoidance of further raids was sheer good luck. The war ended and the people of this deprived area were recipients of the advantages of the social programme of the Attlee government, and this was to play a significant role in the history of the city a quarter of a century later.

Two other places outside of Belfast, both about a dozen miles from the city, were attacked on that same night: Newtownards and Bangor. The former held the only other tactical target outside of Belfast. Its airfield was a staging field for the steady stream of Sunderland seaplanes and Stirling bombers built by Shorts in Dundonald on the city's outskirts. Five servicemen were killed and twenty civilians were wounded by a stick of HE and incendiary bombs. Bangor, as a coastal town, played its part in Western Approaches but the bombs fell, as in Derry, on purely residential streets like Ashley Gardens, killing a mother and two adult daughters of the Grattan family, who lived in Number 40. Other fatalities were Margaret Byers (60) of 5 Hazeldene Gardens and Robert E Wright of 32 Avenue Baylands. In all, seven homes were severely damaged. The local paper, the *County Down Spectator*, believed that 'a large white cinema' was the target mistaken for a strategic building. The cinema was the Troxy but the *Spectator* was too wary of the censor to name it. The *Standard* that reported the Derry bombings with such pathos on 18 April carried on the next page seven column inches about the Bangor raid with the noncommittal headline: 'Coast Town Raided.' It reported six deaths and told of 'a large delayed-action bomb' that fell in the garden of a schoolmaster's garden making a crater fifteen feet deep and wide, and requiring the evacuation of people from 'a considerable area'. Newtownards, six miles away, was not mentioned.

By the standards of raids in Britain and, later in the war in Germany and Japan, the 'country' raids probably do deserve the epithet 'slight' used to describe them by John Blake in his official history; Robert Fisk relegates all three to a short footnote in his *In Time of War* and at least three extant chronicles of World War II do not mention the raids in Northern Ireland at all. Compared with Coventry, Dresden or Hiroshima, they were slight indeed. The trauma, however, was to persist and it was not until VE Day (8 May 1945) that people throughout the north slept without a trace of unease. The Royal Naval authorities in Derry expected the Luftwaffe to return and put what pressure they could on the War Office to improve the city's defences. The number of heavy ack-ack guns was increased to twenty-eight and the lighter Bofors to fourteen. Within a few weeks there were thirty-two barrage balloons making the city and port the best defended of any town in the United Kingdom. It was simply that Hitler's intended rapid conquest of Russia did not materialise that saved the city, which had become a much more strategic target with the entry of the United States and the presence there of all varieties of American forces. The *Wehrmacht* were stopped at Stalingrad and Derry was saved. For Belfast the last, worst raid was still to come. Less than three weeks after the previous visitation, the German air force returned and tried to obliterate the city by fire.

9

The Great Fire of Belfast

IN BELFAST THE SLOW CLEARING UP BEGAN, made excessively difficult by the condition of even the main roads, to say nothing of the warren of small streets with houses that in Donegal, Connemara or Kerry would in the old days have earned them the description 'congested districts'. Clearing up was heartbreaking, not only for its evidence of domestic evisceration, walls torn down to reveal poor kitchens and 'good rooms' kept for Sundays and visitors with bits of Chesterfield suites, plants and broken souvenirs of Bangor and the Isle of Man. The rubble also revealed further bodies now in noisome stages of decomposition. Those who had survived the destruction of their houses tended by daylight to haunt the sites hoping to recover personal treasures. Others, noted more for rapacity than concern, engaged in widespread looting. One victim of an air raid who had been a publican returned to his bar to find that not only had his stock of liquor been removed but the thieves had also unscrewed the brass fittings. One of the sadder aspects of the ditchers was that they tended to bring their most precious possessions nightly to their lairs and occasionally revealed odd priorities. Photographs of loved ones in frames were understandable but some brought often unwieldy clocks and even flower vases. Some more fastidious than others brought nightware as well as nightwear.

One piece of necessary cruelty was the disposal of the animals in the Zoological Gardens at Bellevue. MacDermott answered tearful criticism that the shooting was necessary in case fear-maddened beasts released by bombs from their cages or enclosures would become a hazard to those who lived within a lion's roar of Hazelwood. The *Belfast News Letter* of Monday, 21 April reported under the headline 'Zoo Animals Shot' that 'thirty-three animals at Bellevue Zoo were shot last Saturday'. A McLain MRCVS, the vet in charge of all veterinary aspects of ARP, told the reporter that he understood the pang many people would suffer, especially the head keeper Dick Foster and his staff. The shooting was done by a sergeant in the LDV (Local Defence Volunteers), later the Home Guard, called EV Murray, and by a Constable Thomas Ward from Glengormley, who had been a marksman with the Irish Guards during the Great War. The list included five lions, two lionesses, two cubs, five bears (one black, two brown and two polar), six wolves, a tiger, a hyena, a puma, a lynx, a giant rat, a vulture and two racoons. It was a bloody slaughter but unavoidable to prevent the danger of such a menagerie being accidentally let loose on Cave Hill and the greenery of the Upper Antrim Road.

Whatever reassurance this culling may have given to the residents of the area it also implied a continued threat of more raids to come. The ditching continued with the same volume and increased intensity. The dazzlingly white, stately parliament building at Stormont was coated with pitch to make it a less obvious target and diminish its use as a guide to the Victoria Docks and Shorts. Approaches to the complex were covered in cinders to make progress on them more difficult. Inevitably there was more concern about the fate of the Carson statue; that problem preoccupied not only the cabinet but the majority parliament until a satisfactory solution was found. Andrews got in touch with Carson's widow and was reassured by her that Merrifield, the original sculptor, had retained his cast of the head. The statue was then cocooned with protective sandbags.

MacDermott had trouble getting the geriatric cabinet to concentrate on essentials. He knew how low the reputation of his masters (and himself by the tradition of cabinet responsibility) had sunk. The inadequacy of the city council was a general topic of conversation and now the government were being referred to in a similar vein. He kept up a continuous correspondence with the War Office, asking for more ack-ack, as well as more and better systems of protection: barrage balloons, smoke screens, increased fire-fighting equipment, especially pumps.

The trouble was that Belfast's hour of maximum danger coincided with Britain's direst crisis. Her own cities were attacked from the air with a greater intensity than ever and she could ill afford to grant MacDermott's perfectly reasonable if a trifle tardy request for defensive weapons. Some guns arrived from Britain and a number were moved from Larne and Derry, depleting the armament of those ports. More barrage balloons stations were set up, the number of smoke screen machines increased and much needed searchlight batteries were dispatched from Britain. The Easter raid had both increased and depleted the civil defence force; some in a wave of determination after what they experienced in the raid were anxious to volunteer but this increase was offset by the numbers who left their posts and joined the stream of refugees. These were automatically dismissed. The greatest need was for properly equipped fire-fighters. John Smith, who had led the city's fire-fighting service had, as we have seen, made no attempt to liaise, let alone train the volunteer AFS. He suffered a complete moral and physical breakdown during Easter Week and was lucky to have been allowed to resign, bitterly resenting the decision, on grounds of 'ill-health'. His replacement, Ben White, had been chief of the AFS and had had some experience of fighting blitz fires in England, bringing two parties of AFS men to experience the extreme conditions for themselves. Attachment equipment ordered by MacDermott in October 1940 still hadn't arrived. With a view to improving the protection of civilians the government raised the level of PLV house valuation for the supply of free Anderson shelters from £13 to £29 and this meant that permission had been granted for the erection of 26,000 new shelters. In the bureaucratic incompetence that was characteristic of the time, though the steel fabric for the internal Morrison shelters arrived in quantity, the bolts for their assembly did not fit.

These frantic measures, to those who were aware of them, were an obvious indication that the Luftwaffe would return. It became clear that the Germans' latest policy of bombing raids on ports like Belfast must surely figure again on the visitors' list. A contemporary Luftwaffe document, the original in the Imperial War Museum in London, is reprinted in Brain Barton's book. It gave more detail and was meant as an extension of the July report mentioned earlier. It is a typical piece of German efficiency, a type of early *Vorsprung durch Technik*, only in this case the Nazi superiority came from intelligence technique and the organisational ability of its military bureaucracy. The document is headed: *Nur für den Dienstgebrauch* ('For service use only') and its title is *Zielstammkarte* ('Target list'). Two main targets are named: *Schiffswerft Harland & Wolff Ltd* with Short & Harland Aircraft Factory as next in importance. There follows a detailed verbal description of where precisely the dry docks, the assembly shops, were to be found not only with compass directions but in their relation to each other's position. Attention was directed to the utilities with specific instructions to sabotage them. The whole was an impeccable blueprint for the precision bombing of Belfast's significant contribution to the war effort. Meteorological difficulties and imperfect map-reading may have made the Easter raid less than successful but this time there was going to be no errors.

Bits of this exact information, passed deliberately to *Reichssender Hamburg*, allowed Lard Haw-Haw to name areas that would be targeted in the coming raids. His nightly broadcasts introduced in his refined if slightly ersatz English accent with the words, 'Germany Calling; Germany Calling', first generously promised that he would give the Belfast people time to bury their dead. 'Tuesday was only a sample.' One of the promised targets was the city centre in Derry and he was able to describe a huge golden teapot that hung above McCullagh's, a large Derry grocery.

Instinct that there was more terror to come kept the numbers of ditchers high. Belfast was beginning to assume the appearance of a plague spot. The Group Theatre was closed and attendances at the Opera House and cinemas were very poor. The suburban roads and streets had the appearance of early Sunday mornings. April ended and spring blossomed. The weather was fine and, as people rose two hours earlier because of DBST, they would have appreciated, if they had known, what their adversaries used to say about such mornings: '*Morgenstund' hat Gold im Mund*' – 'The morning hour has gold in its mouth', the German equivalent of 'The early bird catches the worm.' During the last fortnight of April there were almost daily alerts but no planes appeared and no bombs fell. With the instinctive craving for things to be normal the mood of those left in Belfast began slowly to lighten. Maybe the terror was past; maybe the threat was gone.

Sunday, 4 May was a typical late spring day – misty morning, clearing away to a warm afternoon and a clear evening with a moon in the first quarter. Just before ten o'clock, as the slow northern twilight began, a Luftwaffe bombing force left airfields in northern France with the Belfast harbour estate and the Island as their prime targets. When they reached the Irish coast they split into two echelons, one circling over the Copeland Islands to approach the city from the northeast along the north shore of the lough, the other following the previous raiders' route by Carlingford, Hilltown and Dromara approaching the city from the south. The effect was that of the classical 'pincer movement' that meant attack from two directions, south and northeast. The bombers were part of an air armada of 471 planes, mainly Junkers Ju88s and Heinkel HE111s, that intended to bomb (again) Liverpool and Barrow-in-Furness, a shipbuilding and industrial town in north Lancashire. For at least 150 of these bombers the docks, shipyards and plane factories of Belfast were their targets for that night. This time there was no doubt about the success of their mission. Conditions for the task were perfect. There were no meteorological complications, a clear night with a quarter-moon, and the city a replica of all the intelligence photographs, only clearer. There was no absolute need to drop flares and the smokescreen generated at 11.30pm by the newly installed machines could hide but not protect the already pin-pointed targets. Some smarter than usual operations chief in occupied Europe had realised that incendiaries actually did more damage and lasted longer in their effect than other kinds of bomb, like HE and parachute mines.

This attack was intended to start a firestorm and it succeeded with the pouring down on the docks area of nearly 100,000 incendiaries. More than 220 tons of HE bombs followed, the targets clearly illuminated by the fires. The incendiaries could not penetrate the ground but the other cocktail of HE, paramines and oil-bombs did complementary damage to the water mains and sewers. Even if the combined city and auxiliary services had had sufficient trained manpower they had nothing to fill their hoses. Some resourceful fire-fighters remembered that the hidden urban river, the Farset, lay underneath High Street. They were able to reach the flow and pump some water from there until the tide began to ebb. The same ploy was used in the Newtownards Road, again the scene of much domestic destruction, by tapping into the Connswater stream but it too failed as the tide went out. The other source was the city's main river, the Lagan, but until the voluntary appliances from Dundalk and Dublin arrived, having been summoned at 2.20, they lacked the equipment to reach it.

The sorties flew in at between 7,000 and 9,000 feet, just enough to keep their flight-paths above the strengthened balloon barrage. The Luftwaffe planes had shown up on radar screens at about a quarter to one on the Monday morning but the ack-ack batteries had been mobilised from midnight. Most of the bombs were aimed visually, except where the smokescreen had obscured the important targets; then the bombardiers relied on the navigators' maps, aerial photographs and elementary mathematics. The docks and shipyards bore the brunt of the attack. The fabric of the Harland & Wolff yard was weak and highly flammable, and the firm had no fixed protocol for dealing with the situation. The result was that the fires started by the devices spread rapidly and in fact there was no need of the incendiary saturation that the Island endured. The dry night wind and the wooden structures that served as temporary workshops and stores assisted in the conflagrations. With typical bureaucratic efficiency fires were graded according to intensity as 'conflagrations' (major fires that were spreading rapidly), 'major fires' (those requiring the attention of thirty pumps), 'serious fires' (fires requiring more than eleven pumps but less than thirty) and 'small fires'. Fires of these categories were listed in order after the raid: two conflagrations, twenty-two major fires, fifty-eight serious fires and 125 small fires.

The HEs helped spread the conflagrations and in some dramatic cases caused the sections of the collapsing buildings to become deadly 'ground-to-ground' missiles; steel sheets sent frisbying through the air, timber struts as thick as telegraph-poles javelining through the night sky, in one case demolishing an empty air-raid shelter. The fixed wharfs of the docks burned quickly but it became clear to the pilots and the *Luftwaffenmajore* that the incendiaries were not as totally destructive of the ships at various stages of construction in the dry docks. It was decided to boost the fire-bombs with mines, primed as usual to explode at surface level. The initiative was successful; three corvettes moored in the Musgrave Channel, almost ready for fitting, were destroyed and the *Fair Head,* a transport ship lying in the Dufferin Dock with a cargo of essential military supplies, was broken in two by a paramine and the wreck blocked the entrance for some months. The intention to wound Belfast's industrial capacity was effectively realised. The worst hit was Harland & Wolff with most of the structures razed, drawing offices, extensive sheds, engine works and repair shops crisped. The most debilitating attack was suffered by the electrical shop, the heart of the enterprise, so seriously damaged that it took three months to repair. So great was the damage and so traumatised the workforce that the yard remained idle for forty-eight hours. Seventy-seven different areas were designated damaged and nine unexploded bombs had first to be dealt with before the slow tidying-up operation could begin. It was little wonder that the shipyards took six months to return to full production.

Shorts aircraft factory, a mile to the northeast, was saturated with incendiaries that did so much damage that no night work was possible in the plant for over a year. Two planes were destroyed and others damaged but Shorts on the whole fared better than the shipyard. The lack of essential night opening in the factory was caused by the difficulty of blacking out the scattered complex.

Because of their proximity to the shipyards and plane factories the streets on both sides of the river caught the collateral fire. York Street, as well as being bombarded, was strafed by cannon fire from the gunners in the German planes. The main area of civilian damage was an irregular shape with its southern boundary stretching west from roughly the intersection of the Beersbridge and Newtownards Roads as far as the Royal Victoria Hospital at the top of the Grosvenor Road, and taking in streets to the south as far as Shaftesbury Square. On the other side of the docks area, bombs fell between the Limestone and Cliftonville Roads. It may have been a deliberately confined area, concentrating on ships and shipyard, but there was clearly an element of economic targeting in that the city centre, that had partially escaped before, now took its beating in turn: Royal Avenue, Donegall Place, Donegall Square, Bedford Street, Dublin Road, and the many small linking streets between Great Victoria Street and Dublin Road. The northern end of Royal Avenue and its feeder streets took the greatest hammering. Donegall Street, Rosemary Street, Victoria Street, Skipper Street and North Street looked after the raid like human mouths, riddled with caries and showing only a few decaying stumps. Bridge Street had been totally reduced to rubble.

Not all the destruction was confined to the designated saturation area. A bomb fell in the Beechmount area behind St Mary's College, wiping out three families. The target, if deliberate, was probably Mackies foundry that, in fact, sustained only minimal damage and hardly faltered in its production schedule. The women and children, Catholic and Protestant, nearly 300 in number, who had taken shelter in the crypt of Clonard monastery were terrified when a bomb falling close by blew open the door that led to the street level. One of the Redemptorist priests, Fr Tom Murphy, appeared immediately wearing a steel helmet and gave a general absolution of lifetime sins to all in the monastery's care. It would have surely consoled the Catholic refugees but may have caused some spiritual ambivalence to the Protestants. The priests themselves found shelter in the kitchen cellar. When the All Clear sounded shortly after half-past four the survivors walked stiff-legged into a morning red with dawnlight but long before the real dawn. The city was blazing. The ditchers on the hills and parks believed that the whole city centre was gone as were the docks and the other elements of the industrial estate. To the east fires raged apparently without control and those with a sense of topography understood that the Holy Week raid had been re-run this time to diabolically greater effect.

Charlie Gallagher, who had attended the fatalities in Messines Park in Derry, his native town, during Easter Week, was one of six volunteers from the Civil Defence force to travel with ambulances to give what help they could. Not all those who volunteered were permitted to travel because it was feared that Derry might be next. When he reached the top of Glenshane Pass from which the whole of east Ulster may be viewed as on a map, he stopped his overheating ambulance and got out to stretch his legs. He could see the usually dull sheen of Lough Neagh blaze with orange light and further to the east the fires that, in the confusion of thermals and tricks of the light, seemed to pulse like a fiery heart. The crump and hiss of falling bombs though distant were clearly audible as were the broken sounds of German planes, a sound he had first heard eighteen days before back home. When he got to Antrim the air was thick with what Ulster people call 'colly', a choking mixture of ash and coal dust that was an unlooked-for side product of the Great Fire. He had to stop and scrape the noxious grit from his windscreen and side mirrors before making his way the seventeen miles into the urban inferno. He afterwards realised that there was little he could do. This third raid was far beyond the capacity of Civil Defence to control. He was sent to the Short Strand area to carry the bombed-out families to reception centres. He was appalled by the condition of his refugees, unwashed, terrified, badly dressed and inert. Like many other ebullient people he had had no idea that such conditions existed and he was conscious of his own inability to do much to help. He returned home that Monday afternoon deeply depressed and concerned about how Derry might cope with a similar catastrophe.

One of the first victims of the Holy Week curtain raiser was St Patrick's Church of Ireland Church on the Newtownards Road. It suffered its third attack on 5 May and was left an incomplete set of crumbling walls. Other heavily damaged streets in the area between the Newtownards Road and Sydenham were Avondale Street, Chater Street, Witham Street, Westcott Street, Hornby Street, Ravenscroft Street, Bryson Street, Mersey Street, Tower Street, Donegore Street (now no longer with us) and Tamar Street. This area was attacked again the following night in a kind of epilogue raid by aircraft, straying from a force intent on pulverising Clydeside. Forty-seven people died in direct hits on shelters in Ravenscroft Avenue, Donegore Street and Avondale Street. Yet, in Hornby Street, although the shelter was partially damaged by a paramine, the seventeen occupants survived, and despite an HE bomb leaving a large crater in Chater Street, less than forty feet from another crowded shelter, there were no casualties. As would later be realised the death toll from the Great Fire was only two-ninths of that of the Easter raid. MacDermott took this to be proof of the efficacy of his shelters and indeed greater use of them was made than previously, but a more persuasive argument was that more than 100,000 Belfast citizens had left town and thousands more had ditched as soon as the alert sounded. MacDermott was less enthusiastic about a rising tide of opinion that the shelters were either badly designed or that the builders had not followed correct specifications.

Tower Street, called after the square front of St Patrick's, was, as we have seen, one of many, non-tactical targets to be badly damaged. One of its inhabitants, the six-year-old Sam McCready, for many years an important member of Mary O'Malley's Lyric Theatre company, joined the flock of refugees who sought safety in the country. In his memoir *Baptism of Fire* (2007), subtitled 'My Life with Mary O'Malley and the Lyric Players', he describes their first flight into the village of Culcavey, County Down, less than a mile from Hillsborough, where his sister's husband had relatives. His mother and seven children spent a few crowded nights with these remote in-laws. The father made his way back each day into the city to his work while Mrs McCready, with desperate determination, looked for other, less crowded accommodation. Her son tells how she walked up the steep hill past Government House and out the Dromore Road knocking on every door to try to find shelter for her family, asking, 'Have you a place to rent?' She had no success, partly because many refugees had already been billeted there, and also because a working-class family with seven children from the Newtownards Road in east Belfast was not as welcome as the flowers of spring. Taking a side road that led to one of Ireland's many Ballygowans she found what she sought at Taughblane Orange Hall. It was small, with a tiny kitchen and one large room, eventually partitioned to sleep the McCreadys. Sam went to the local school, learned country skills and lore, and, young as he was, realised that there was a perhaps better life for lads away from the city.

He was one of the lucky ones. The number of casualties may have been considerably smaller than that associated with the Easter Week raid but the displaced and the temporary ditchers, accounting for respectively fifty percent and six percent of the population, had to face fear, discomfort, alienation and humiliation. (Figures are approximate, gleaned from Ministry of Home Affairs reports, and extrapolated from the 1937 census returns.) They could not have known that the May raids would be the last ghastly visitation. The raid of 5–6 May was, as it turned out, the Luftwaffe's last hurrah in the west. A single reconnaissance plane flew over the city on Tuesday, 6 May to obtain photographic evidence of the damage inflicted – necessary for the relentless and highly effective propaganda machine run by Joseph Goebbels (1897–1945). That evening two planes, part of a strike force aimed at the shipyards on the Clyde in Scotland, were either diverted away from the target area because of bad weather or, having strayed from the pack, mistook Belfast for their target. (The parallels with the Derry raid are striking: one and two planes, no longer part of a larger force, attack weapons, paramines, little damage done and an approximately equal number of fatal casualties.) At a quarter to one on Wednesday, 6 May mines were dropped again on east Belfast, the planes drawn to a supposed target by the still blazing fires especially in the Belfast Rope Works. Fourteen people died, forty were seriously injured and 300 made homeless. One can only try to imagine the sense of fear, nausea and disappointment felt by Belfast people on the front line when two and a quarter hours later the bombers returned to shower the same location with more fire-bombs. In the weeks – the quiet weeks – that followed, fear turned to anger and heads were made to roll.

10

What the Papers Said

IT IS HARD FOR US, LIVING in our global village with instant communications, to understand how cagey even the local papers were in their reporting of the details of the raids. As we have discovered in a previous chapter the *Derry Journal* reporting the city's one bruising brush with the Luftwaffe put the story on page eight of its Friday edition, three days in arrears. It had gone to bed too early on the Tuesday evening with Wednesday's paper – it appeared tri-weekly – to report the landmine damage in Derry, but made their lead story Bishop Neil Farren's address at the Féis. The town had been unable to talk of anything else but the paper's headline read: 'Raid on Six County Town'. The terms 'Six County'/'Six Counties' were invariably used by the nationalist paper to show non-recognition of Northern Ireland.

Their coverage the day after the first raid on Belfast on the Tuesday of Holy Week was headed: 'First Raid on Six Counties' with sub-heads 'Waves of German Bombers Attack Town', 'Terrific A.A. Barrage' and 'Ten Bodies So Far Recovered'. The second paragraph began with a phrase that was to become a slug for all the papers. (A slug in those days of hot-metal printing presses was a strip of metal already composed and to hand in storage because of its frequent use by reporters.) 'Fires were caused' was the phrase and the paper's reporter elaborated with the news that between forty and fifty buildings, including a church – St Patrick's in Ballymacarret – had been damaged. The correspondent told the story of James Kirkwood, who roused his children when the raid began and got them to shelter under the kitchen table. He was standing with his wife in the scullery when an HE bomb blew away the whole front of the house and the kitchen ceiling fell on top of them. They were eventually dug out of the debris by ARP wardens. Another family called Watson, whose story was also told in the *Journal*, had been shepherded out of the bomb-damaged house and taken to a temporary shelter. It caught fire and they had to be removed again to a street shelter that in turn received blast damage. The addresses of the two families interviewed were, of course, not given but unusually the names of the two AFS casualties were. They were Archibald McDonald (25) and Bruce Harkness (30) and it was noted that their unit was called out sixteen times that night to deal with fires started by incendiary bombs. In a box printed in the centre of the column that told these stories was the reminder, not likely fully to be heeded, that blackout times on the Spy Wednesday was 8.45pm to 6.05am.

The *Derry Standard* printed on that same day (Wednesday, 9 April) told much the same story, inevitably since they were dependent on official communiqués but they led with the deliberately down-playing official statements:

> A small force of enemy bombers, one of which was shot down over the sea by our night-fighters and blew up in mid-air attacked an area in Northern Ireland and caused some damage in industrial, commercial and other property. Some casualties were unfortunately caused.

The words 'area in Northern Ireland' are again indicative of the almost paranoiac care to avoid 'giving comfort of information to the enemy'. It was really quite pointless since everybody in Germany from *Wehrmacht* headquarters to the smallest reluctant member of the *Hitlerjugend* knew that the Belfast docks had been hit on the Tuesday night in a sneak raid. The *Belfast Telegraph* was as squeamish about naming names as all the other papers. The *Standard* as a Unionist paper gave an air of enthusiastic participation in the war effort; the *Journal* as the oldest nationalist paper in Ulster maintained a studied detachment, if not quite going to the extent of uttering the mantra, 'Let Britain fight her own wars.'

The oldest Irish paper of all, the *Belfast News Letter* (founded in 1737), had a headline on 8 April in the Late News column, 'Widespread Night Raids', and the piece mentioned several targets but made no mention of Belfast. Perhaps under the censorship rules they had to wait for an official communiqué. The *Belfast Telegraph*, as an evening paper, was able to quote the statement by the Minister of Public Safety – MacDermott – quoted above. The Press Association's coverage was even briefer and less specific: 'Enemy aircraft over a Northern Ireland town. Some bombs were dropped.' On the following day, Wednesday, 9 April, the 'small raid' was the subject of the *News Letter*'s first leader. It regretted that 'Northern Ireland's long immunity from serious air-attack ended yesterday morning with a sharp raid of some hours' duration, during which unfortunately, a number of casualties, some of them fatal, occurred.' It went on to advise readers that since the illusion that Northern Ireland was unlikely to be attacked had been shattered 'the community, as a whole, realising… that other and worse raids may follow, can be expected now to cooperate much more readily with the authorities in precautionary measures.' Though the word 'now' was not italicised the message was clear. Most people had resented and mocked the ARP people for their perhaps inevitable officiousness. Now they had to see them as necessary protectors from the worst of the Blitz.

On the Thursday its Blitz story (on page five) was headed 'Ulster Raider Shot Down: Fighter Pilot's Eleventh "Kill".' It was another success for Squadron-Leader JW Simpson who, in true Biggles spirit, played down his courage:

> I could not hear it [the noise of the Heinkel exploding] above the roar of
> my engine, but my machine was caught in the blast and I was thrown

> about 300 yards upwards and sideways. I soon righted myself and when
> I looked down I saw bits of burning aircraft floating slowly towards the
> sea. I then came home.

The last short sentence was brilliant. The rest of the piece gave a list of casualties. As well as the two AFS men already named the dead also included three fire watchers: Harold Gowan, William Pollock and Daniel Fee; Joseph Lambert, linen lapper; Thomas Bell; Hugh Stewart, fitter; Alexander Hagan, labourer; John Patience, plater; Stanley Kyle; and John Eskdale. The story also reported that fifty centres for the provision of emergency meals had been provided. They were designed to help people who, while not rendered homeless, were unable to cook food in their own houses. Those rendered homeless should go to a rest centre. The amount of wishful thinking packed into those last sentences is remarkable. More honest were the blunt words addressed by the charismatic Presbyterian cleric, the Rev A Wylie Blue, to his May Street congregation at a lunch-hour intercession service: 'Northern Ireland now knew what war was and people had seen the unscrupulous ruthlessness of it.'

On Tuesday, 8 April the *Irish News*, the voice of Ulster constitutional Nationalism since it was founded as an anti-Parnell paper in 1891, gave the raid two columns on its first page with the oddly undramatic leading headline: 'Northern Ireland Area Has Air Raid; Attack by Small Force of German Bombers.' In keeping with the current practice the name of Belfast was nowhere mentioned though those who read the paper outside of the city might guess the location from such sentences as, 'Despite the lateness of the hour there was a considerable number of people in the streets.' The story also noted that the *Irish News* reporter had just vacated a phone box from which he was filing his story when all its glass was shattered by blast. The reporter had allowed himself a little colour in his description:

> Flaming onions [a specific kind of light ack-ack] and tracer shells
> converged in a fiery display, while above all burst the shrapnel from the

> heavier batteries. Shrapnel falling in showers on the streets and rooftops struck sparks from the ground and injured several people running for shelter. A man named William McRory (33) was taken to hospital with shrapnel injuries and shock.

Nowadays it would be called 'collateral damage' or 'friendly fire'. Incidentally, the paper cost one penny, five twelfths of one-pence in today's money.

The following Friday week, 18 April, again on page eight, the *Derry Journal* saw no point in hiding the location of the big raid, though still careful not to admit that Derry too had suffered. Black headlines announced, 'Belfast's Terrible Raid; Deaths Number Almost 200; Tens of Thousands of Bombs Dropped.' It listed among the damaged buildings two churches, a cinema, a library and a hospital. The cinema was the York in York Street, the site of utter saturation bombing; it was never rebuilt. The paper went on to say that the official German News Agency had stated: 'This mass attack on Belfast may be compared in its effect to the heaviest attack, which has hitherto been inflicted on British armaments centres and ports.' This claim had already been contradicted by the *Northern Whig*, then Belfast's other Unionist morning paper, maintaining a slightly more radical agenda than the *News Letter*. On the Thursday morning it had printed a paragraph stating: 'The enemy claim that hundreds of bombers pressed home the attack and declare it was every way as heavy as those directed against armaments centres and ports in Britain. But although industrial premises were damaged, working-class districts took the heaviest battering.'

The third morning paper in the western city, the *Londonderry Sentinel*, made the raids the subject of its editorial for Thursday, 17 April. It, too, was published tri-weekly on the days left free by the *Journal* and *Sentinel* and so was the earliest provincial paper with the story of the Belfast and Derry raids:

> Our Northern Ireland is right in the front line now. On Tuesday night it was made the special object of a Nazi air blitzkrieg, which was of

> widespread character. When Great Britain entered the war the people of Ulster were prepared loyally to share the sacrifices, which that decision involved, and, regardless of cost, they have never wavered in their attachment and devotion to Britain's cause. While there were some people who thought and hoped that German bombers would not visit our shores to rain down death and destruction as they have done in Britain, our leaders and the vast bulk of the community believed otherwise and steeled themselves to any emergency, even if they did not take all the precautions, which such an eventuality would demand.

It is an interesting paragraph, praising and criticising in equal measure while still making the acceptable declaration of loyalty. Of the three accounts given by the Derry 'mornings' it gave the greatest coverage with grisly accounts of individual victims. In a series of short paragraphs, most of only one sentence, it highlighted the horrors. A husband and wife were blown out into the street as they slept and were found twenty yards from their wrecked home, still in bed and dead. A nurses' home attached to a hospital was destroyed by high explosive bombs – this, it transpired, was in Frederick Street, on the site of the old Royal Hospital. 'Pathetic scenes were witnessed as small groups of women and children, some of them still scantily clad, rushed away to a safety zone, taking with them whatever small possessions they had managed to salvage in their hasty get-away.' They also mentioned with mounting horror that a cinema had been completely demolished, a large city store, and two newspaper offices were damaged.

In the city, news coverage grew in the days following the raid. On Wednesday, 16 April, the *News Letter*'s coverage was muted. There were eight single-column inches, most of which were taken up by MacDermott's official communiqué that said very little. Phrases like 'over an area comprising practically the whole of Northern Ireland' were deliberately misleading, and 'Damage has been sustained by some industrial premises, but many of the bombs fell on residential property' was not very enlightening. By Thursday there was an end to caginess. Half-inch headlines announced: 'Hundreds of Bombers

Used in Raid on Belfast.' Bangor, however, was not specified except as 'A Coastal Town' where though many 'baskets' of incendiaries were dropped there was little damaged by fire because of successful cooperation by 'householders, wardens and AFS personnel'. The Tonic Cinema, the town's pride, and not named in the account, gleamed white in the lights of the flares and fires, and many unsuccessful attempts were made to hit it. A delayed-action bomb fell on the nearby golf course 'and made necessary a further precautionary evacuation'. Newtownards, which suffered the attention of the bombers that night, was not even mentioned.

The main story referred, again unspecifically, to a 'tragic triangle' of streets, about which the reporters recorded a total of 'at least two-hundred outbreaks'. Earlier they referred to 'one of the greatest scenes of devastation where a high explosive struck a spinning mill bringing down thousands of tons of masonry which completely buried small working-class dwellings'. They meant the York Street Mill but did not mention the forty-two houses in Sussex Street and Vere Street that were flattened. They also referred, again naming no names, to the fire attack on Ewart's Mill on the Crumlin Road and to the fate of Wilton's large Funeral Parlour nearby that was reduced to a shell. Nor did the paper mention the deaths of all those lovely horses.

The 'Fire Raid' was covered by provincial papers with different degrees of angst and cheerfulness. In the northwest the memories of the Wednesday three weeks before tended to darken any positivity that people tried to show. The *Derry Journal* covered the story of the smaller Tuesday raid in its edition of Wednesday, 7 May. Either the censor was more relaxed or the editor more courageous because the city was named in the paper's headline: 'Over Belfast Again.' Subs told the story in shorthand: 'Another Raid Yesterday Morning'; 'Casualties in Residential Areas'; 'Still Digging for the Dead'; 'Stormont and Refugees.' No topographical details of damage or casualties were given, perhaps because in its slightly exclusivist way its editor felt that his self-conscious local readers had little knowledge and less interest in Belfast streets. The last paragraph reported a characteristically meaningless response by Bates:

> At Stormont the question of refugees was considered and the Minister of Home Affairs, Sir Dawson Bates, gave an assurance that the over-crowding conditions in certain towns and villages due to evacuation was being considered by his Department and they were taking all possible steps to rectify the matter.

On page six (because of paper shortages the *Journal* was only allowed six broadsheet pages per issue), they printed a redaction of an *Irish Times* reporter's account of a visit to Belfast on the Monday. The editorial staff had come to realise the full extent of the damage and gave forty column inches of two-inch width to what was virtually a reprint. The reporter spoke of the contrast between the shining beauty of the rest of the province and the pall of grey smoke over Belfast: 'Outside the city the sun was shining on a sylvan scene; inside it was hell.' It was already clear that the May raids were much more destructive of factories, buildings, docks and shipping but 'it is hoped that the casualty toll will not be as heavy…' The reporter was made uneasy by the signs of what seemed to him a kind of martial law:

> Large areas of the city were cordoned-off and guarded by military… Side streets were cluttered with diverted traffic, the military directed people on different routes, and occasionally the crash of collapsing could be heard above the noise of the army lorries, loaded with the goods and chattels of the homeless, and the more grim tarpaulin-covered cargoes that took another direction.

He was also upset that because of the destruction of street-name plates some native-born Belfast people became lost in their own city. The destruction of 'some of the finest modern buildings' appalled him but he was pleased to record heartfelt appreciation in conversation with 'bandaged firemen and members of the heroic casualty and air raid services, who were heroic in their selfless praise of the fire units and ambulances which came from the South to assist them'. He saw 'the ruins of churches, hotels, great stores and business premises, a railway, big sheds, a distillery, shops and houses, and watched the organised gangs of military workers tackle the terrible task of recovering the dead all over again'. It is clear that this was his first visit north since his list of ruined – and missing – buildings is a conflation of the accumulated destruction from the three raids.

With such a long piece it was hard for the reporter to avoid a repetitive pedestrian account of wrecked fabric and snuffed-out lives. He tried as all journalists do to bring some colour and drama to his dismal story. He noted the four ruined walls of a Presbyterian church outside of which was a notice reading: 'Put your trust in God, as I do,' with the façade concealing 'a completely destroyed interior'. In an early example of *Irish Times* policy of equal space for all creeds he also reported on the destruction 'in another street' of a Methodist church. It was with some relief that 'although the area round a well-known Church of Ireland Cathedral was a blazing inferno the Cathedral itself was undamaged'. What odd sense of decorum prevented him from naming St Anne's in Lower Donegall Street, I wonder; perhaps it too was censored. Failing to find a seriously damaged Catholic church he did the next best thing and reported the complete demolishing 'close to a Catholic church' of a Catholic Young Men's Club. This was almost certainly St Patrick's in Donegall Street but he felt unable to say so.

Other Blitz stories on the same page included a report from the *Belfast News Letter* that described a visit paid by Andrews to inspect 'some of the damage'. His reported words included justly deserved praise of the 'work of the Civil Defence Service and of the magnificent contribution made by the fire fighting services'. This begins to ring hollow when he observes 'that to him it was amazing that they had been able to bring fires under control within such brief periods'. That was precisely what they were unable to do since they had no water for the hoses. The spontaneous mercy dash of Dublin fire appliances and Irish Red Cross ambulances, with stretcher parties, would have been rather more effective if the water mains had not been fractured in sixty-seven different places. The *Journal* also carried 'harrowing stories' culled by Dublin reporters from Belfast refugees, including one of a mother with five children whose house had been partially damaged in the Easter raid. When it was made habitable again they returned only to have the roof blown off and cracks appear in the walls. They ran to the nearest shelter but a bomb demolished a section of it and they saw several people killed by falling masonry. A Mrs Margaret Healy from the Antrim Road had gone to Dublin with her five children after her house was damaged by incendiaries and had just returned on 2 May. She told a reporter that this time she intended to reside in Kerry for the duration. The account ended with the news that Red Cross ambulances met each GNR train from Belfast at Amiens Street to bring those without planned accommodation to the shelter of the Red Cross hostel in Mespil Road.

The *Londonderry Sentinel*, because it published on Tuesdays, again had the story before its rivals, the *Journal* and *Standard*. It talked of the 'usual savagery and murderous hatred' of the 'merciless German bombers' and painted the same picture of death and destruction but tried to end on a positive, if not entirely convincing, note: 'Despite the heavy bombing and the intensity of the barrage the morale of the citizens was of the highest. When their homes, the result of efforts of a lifetime, had either been shattered by high explosive or rendered uninhabitable, they accepted instructions from the wardens with the greatest calm and proceeded to the various rest centres.' Like the *Journal*, the *Derry Standard* led with a short account of the milder Tuesday raid, quoting the joint communiqué of the Northern Ireland Ministry of Home Affairs and RAF headquarters:

A small force of enemy bombers made a short attack on the Belfast area and other Northern Districts early this morning. One aircraft was shot down by our fighters and fell in flames into the sea. During the attack high explosive bombs were dropped. Casualties were comparatively light, although some were unfortunately fatal.

It also carried a paragraph in which the unnamed pilot of a fighter (unspecified but certainly a Hurricane and piloted by the resourceful Squadron-Leader JWC Simpson DFC, chief of 245 Hurricane squadron and Aldergrove's own air ace) described his kill of the JU88. The operation took a mere five seconds. As he soared as fast as he could through light clouds he suddenly saw 'three heavy bombers line astern, clearly silhouetted against the moon'. He did not consciously fire at the first but he *did* fire and he saw it burst into flames and fall nose first into the sea. He took some evasive action but when he was ready to engage again, the other two JU88s were gone.

The North German edition of the official Nazi party newspaper, the *Völkischer Beobachter* ('National Observer'), for Tuesday, 6 May went to town and with reason. Their headline in very black Gothic print screamed, 'Strong and tight formations of warplanes bomb Belfast.' Beside the story it printed a terrifying picture of huge flames and clouds of smoke on both sides of the Lagan. The story claimed that Belfast shipyard and industry had been completely smashed. The next day it printed a boxed story from *Kriegsberichter* ('war correspondent') Christoph von der Ropp with the headline: '*Brände an allen Ecken und Enden*' –'Fires on every corner and street end.' Von der Ropp had travelled with the Luftwaffe to Belfast in the last wave of the bombers after *Kampfgruppe 100*, the crack pathfinder section, had lit the whole sky up with 6,000 incendiaries: 'Eventually Belfast came into view, a pulsing kaleidoscope of lights in many colours, of white, yellow and red, sending waves of smoke over the whole city. There were hundreds of lesser and greater fires that we could clearly discern. Under a thick pall of smoke in the docks the oil terminal was an inferno…' There was much more of this inevitably triumphalist stuff; the raid had been a glowing success in every sense. By comparison the *Belfast News Letter*'s first report was sober but stoical: 'Big Raid On Belfast; Many Great Fires Started; Heavy Casualties.' Further down it admitted: 'It is feared that casualties will be heavy. Further details will be announced later in the day.'

The minor Tuesday raid, the last on Belfast, was not, as we've seen, the last in Ireland. The *Derry Journal* carried a story on Friday, 7 May, again deep in the lower recesses of page six. Under the head, 'Bomb Dropped in Donegal', it told how, at the farm of Patrick Douglas at Carthage Hill, Coolkenny, a bomb had left a crater twenty-four feet in diameter and ten feet deep. Injuries were slight, Douglas receiving a few abrasions to his face. The Irish government office protested to Hempel but took no further action. It became a kind of preview for the Dublin raid at the very end of the month. *The Irish Times* (then costing two old pence) led with the story of the Dublin bombing on Monday, 2 June 1941. Its deliberately pedestrian chief headline – Frank Aiken's censorship board was much more rigorous than its British equivalent – 'German Bombs Were Dropped On Dublin' was followed by subheads: 'Government Protest To Be Made In Berlin'; 'Dead Number 30'; 'Injured Over 80.' The story began with a reprint of an official statement:

> The Government regrets to announce that as a result of the bombs dropped in Dublin during the early hours of Saturday morning at least 27 lost their lives and about 80 received injuries. Considerable damage to houses was caused. A further bomb was dropped near Arklow on Sunday morning. No lives were lost but there was some damage to property.
>
> Investigations having shown that the bombs dropped were of German origin, the Charge d'Affaires in Berlin is being directed to protest, in the strongest terms, to the German Government against the violation of Irish territory, and to claim compensation and reparation for the loss of life, the injuries suffered and the damage to property. He is being further directed to ask for definite assurances that the strictest instructions will be given to prevent the flight of aircraft over Irish territory and territorial waters.

The admonition about 'territorial waters' was a little hollow when even the very *Hunde* in *Unter den Linden* knew that that was precisely the way that the bombers found their relatively safe way to Belfast, noting that when there were no further lights to be seen that they must have crossed the border into County Down or County Armagh.

Another sub-head read: 'Many people still missing.' Underneath were printed the names of the twenty-nine people unaccounted for. Those with information were asked to ring Area Warden PJ MacDonagh or any Garda station. The paper carried appeals from the Irish Red Cross Society and the St John Ambulance Brigade who had made themselves responsible for the welfare of the victims, especially the 300 who had been made homeless. It was able to report that already £4,000 had been received from Joseph McGrath (1888–1966), £3,000 from the Hospitals Sweepstake Trust, the charitable institution that he managed, and a personal cheque for £1,000. By odd coincidence, four columns in on the front page is a single column with the headline, 'Dublin Houses Collapse', and a subhead, 'Three Persons Killed.' It describes how two tenement houses in Old Bride Street collapsed on the Sunday morning and the ARP rescue party was diverted from their work at the North Strand. It was an entirely fortuitous event but it added to the gloom of an already miserable weekend.

As one reads the contemporary papers, especially the provincial press, one is impressed by the standard of English in the reports, rather better than that shown by today's journalists, and a kind of detachment about the reporting of local air raids as though they were somehow intrusive, detached from the real world. This was partly due to the strict censorship laws, based practically on the principle: if you won't censor your own work, we'll do it for you. Rather than submit to the inconvenience and tedium of submitting material to an often subjective external censor, editorial staffs preferred not to risk the ministrations of officialdom and imposed their own strictures. In many matters the petty officials generated by the emergency could be mean-spirited and became notorious for their parrot-cry: 'Don't you know there's a war on?' They did carry more international news than the papers of today but their hearts were happier in reporting real news like 'Argus's' selections for Phoenix Park or that 'At last! Here is the film you've been longing to see: Charlie Chaplin in *The Great Dictator* on in the local picture house.' True they gave the 'Black-

Out Times' – the day after the 'Fire Raid' in Belfast, the blinds and shutters did not have to be in place until 10.49pm and were to stay there until 4.53am. In the merry month of May there were barely six hours of darkness and so that was the time of necessary ditching in those late spring nights.

11

After the Blitz

THERE WERE NO FURTHER RAIDS AFTER those of May 1941 but it took time for the bruised and war-scarred people of Belfast to return to normal. Ditching continued for several years until after the Normandy landings of June 1944, and even then there was unease because of the success of the new German rockets, the V1 and the V2, which had brought a second blitz to London and southeast England, killing 53
,000 people. These *Vergeltungswaffen* (retaliation weapons) were unmanned missiles and were very hard to track and counter. But that the Allies' early successes in Europe had them capture the factories where the V-weapons were manufactured, the war in Europe would have dragged on much longer with great loss of life and destruction of property, not only in southern England but also in liberated France and the Low Countries. The V2 could deliver a tonne of HE and had a range of 320 kilometres. In spite of these peripheral concerns, by 1944 the endemic hysteria about air raids had subsided somewhat and Belfast was abuzz with the presence of exotic American troops who caused the innate stiffness of the city to soften.

By then the Blitz debris had been cleared away and the city had a representative share of bomb sites, offering new vistas of surviving buildings, and in late summer, was rich with rose-bay willow-herb (in the circumstances more appropriately called by its alternative term, fireweed) and ragwort that the locals knew as 'benweed', that was often used to decorate the door lintels on May Day.

Because of the way Belfast had developed over the centuries as market town and industrial city, most of the Luftwaffe targets – mills, ropeworks, docks, shipyards, aircraft factories – were concentrated at or near the centre of the city on both sides of the Lagan. The workers in the heavy industries had lived literally in the shadow of the dark satanic mills, as the few survivors of Sussex and Vere Streets knew only too well. For this reason York Street showed great signs of destruction, as did the thoroughfares off York Road to the north. In the city centre destruction was oddly selective. The City Hall, that gorgeous Edwardian wedding-cake, got off relatively lightly. The elaborate banqueting hall, with its fine plasterwork ceiling, lay open to the sky, with damage to walls and roof. St Anne's Anglican Cathedral in Lower Donegall Street escaped serious damage while all the buildings from York Street right to its door were obliterated, including the famous International Bar; the huge site is now occupied by the Belfast campus of the University of Ulster. By sad contrast with St Anne's, Belfast First Presbyterian Church in Rosemary Street, less than twenty-five metres away, was badly damaged.

The city centre street that received the greatest pounding was one of the oldest in Belfast in the sense that there had been a High Street since the place had the nerve to call itself a town. A trio of 'before-and-after' photographs published in the *Belfast Telegraph* and reproduced in its handbook *Bombs on Belfast* (1941) shows High Street in its pre-raid prime as one of the city's premier shopping streets busy with tramcars and terminated by the Albert Memorial, a Gothic clock tower standing at the junction of Queen's Square and Victoria Street. It was designed by WJ Barre (1830–67), though the monopolising and devious Lanyon tried to steal the contract from him. The second picture of the trio shows the street on the morning after the raid, its left-hand side retaining only heaps of rubble and the dangerous shells of once multi-storeyed buildings. Through the artificially created yellow stour, a product of the impregnation of the atmosphere with the dust of a million bricks, one can still see the clock tower. In the third photograph taken after the clear-up, the street is busy as ever with the clock still sentinel at its foot and a large open area bounded by Waring Street, Skipper Street and Church Lane. The space became known as Blitz Square and it was used as a kind of wartime 'it's-happening-now' museum, with examples of barrage balloons, Stirling bombers and tanks regularly on display, especially during 'Save for Victory' campaigns. The large space also served as a military car park, a site for redundant air-raid shelters and huge static water tanks, filthy, dangerous and of interest only to young children. When no police or service personnel were about, the kids sailed toy boats there or doused their mates with water scooped in the hand. In the bitter winter of 1944, all the EWS tanks froze over and another risky game was developed as hardy kids tried to walk on the ice. Once an errant swan rested briefly on a tank in North Queen Street. Thanks, if that is the appropriate word, to the Luftwaffe, central Belfast had now many open spaces and so it remained for many years, a bleak reminder of the spring of '41.

Though both sides preened themselves on their ability at precision bombing the result was, in the city centre, oddly selective. York Street was severely attacked and heavily damaged but the large Belfast Cooperative Store received no more than minimal blast damage while the east side of the street along with parts of Donegall Street, Little and Great Patrick Street and Great George's Street were erased. A single shop opposite the Co-op, solitary in the cleared space, still continued, one might almost say cheekily, to do business. Further north, where Whitla Street met York Road, was the location of the LMS/NCC station that served trains that plied the busy commuter route on the west coast of Belfast Lough to Whitehead and Larne, and from Whiteabbey west towards Antrim and the north coast. The station buildings had sustained some damage during the April bombings but in the Great Fire of 4–5 May it and the Bangor and County Down terminus, its companion across the Lagan, were badly damaged, causing even greater transport chaos. The station frontage looked as if it had been shelled and the glass covers of the platforms, the goods and marshalling yards were hit. The most obvious casualty was the grand LMS hotel that was completely destroyed.

One of the claims made by extremists was that Protestant houses and churches in particular were the main targets for the highly selective German raiders. It is a matter of fact that no Catholic churches were seriously damaged and none, not even the tiny St Joseph's in the dock area, destroyed. A bomb did leave a deep, water-filled crater in the grounds of St Matthew's Catholic Church in Bryson Street, and though the houses all round the Church of the Holy Family at Newington were destroyed, the church appeared undamaged. Yet years later, when the diocese fabric committee recommended refurbishment, it was found that the church was structurally unsound and it was levelled. *Bombs on Belfast* has a section on burning churches, with graphic pictures of Crumlin Road Presbyterian Church, one showing an ARP stretcher party in silhouette, outlined against the burning inferno. One of the earliest victims of the raids was the Anglican St Patrick's Parish Church in Ballymacarrett, which was left a mere shell on the first raid on the morning of Tuesday in Holy Week. It was destroyed by incendiaries that burned through the pitch-pine roof. Soon the old gallery, pews and wooden floor, and the ARP station that had been based in a Sunday School room in the building, were ablaze. The church when reconstructed still bore the scorch marks of the fiery destruction. The proud square tower still stood but the street to which it gave its name was obliterated.

Other places of worship that were destroyed or left as hollow shells were Spamount Congregational Church at the corner of North Queen Street; Oldpark Presbyterian Church, Cliftonville Road; St Barnabas Parish Church, Duncairn Gardens; York Street Presbyterian Church;

York Street Non-Subscribing Presbyterian Church; Castleton Presbyterian Church, York Road; Duncairn Gardens Methodist Church; St James's Parish Church, Antrim Road; St Silas's Parish Church, Oldpark Road; Clifton Street Presbyterian Church; Newington Presbyterian Church; Macrory Memorial Presbyterian Church, Antrim Road; Newtownards Road Methodist Church; and the city centre Rosemary Street Presbyterian Church. Most of them had been built in that part of north Belfast that had been attacked in all three of the big raids.

The Belfast Blitz had two unexpected extra casualties: the prime minister and the Belfast Corporation. The first, John Miller Andrews, was ousted as leader of the government, though formally allowed to resign. Members of the second carried even greater responsibility for the debased state of 'the submerged tenth', but it was other accusations, more precise than the disseminated responsibility for failure of welfare care, that led to their undoing.

Andrews had been a minister since the foundation of the state and when Craigavon died he was heir apparent. Having served the new state worthily, if unimaginatively, he was too old – seventy-two when he resigned – to run a region at war. He was the siege mentality personified, obsessed with the disloyalty of Roman Catholics whose only preoccupation 'was to put us all into the Free state'. With no sense of the divisive nature of the Northern Ireland state nor any conception of in what low esteem his government was held, he would not listen to criticism even from members of his own cabinet and believed firmly in his own words when, in October 1941, he said the position of his government was 'stronger than it had been for years'. Three months before this blinkered statement, on 25 July, the air-raid warning sirens had caused 30,000 Belfast people to rush from the city though no planes came and no bombs fell. The people had lost all trust in both national and local government. A by-election in the hitherto safe Unionist seat of Willowfield was won in December by the maverick Harry Midgley of the Northern Ireland Labour Party and it shook Andrews severely; he observed to Spender that a general election (out of the question in wartime) might cause the government to lose its majority.

Even so he was incapable of taking steps to ameliorate the situation. He would make no move against his incompetent fellows. A kind of sentimental loyalty to the safe, if uncritical, hands of the old guard who had seen the new state successfully into existence prevented the resolute action needed. Typical behaviour was that of the irascible and paranoiac Bates, who lived in Portrush and ran up a mileage of over 30,000 a year in his chauffeur-driven official car – this at a time when petrol was all but unavailable to the public. As Minister of Home Affairs, Bates was responsible for overall security and made no attempt to cooperate well with the talented MacDermott.

Andrews as head of state should have led the way in the prosecution of Belfast Corporation on charges of corruption and patronage, established by an inquiry report in June 1941. There had been a shady land deal over the site for a tuberculosis sanatorium at Whiteabbey but the guilt of incompetence and mismanagement, not to say complacency, of the city fathers was made manifest by the lines of underfed, sickly city children as they queued up for food and delousing in the emergency centres. His sloth in acting was compounded with the guilt of the poor performance of his government and the fact that some of his friends were leading members of the Corporation. He was also held responsible for serious labour troubles that might have been toughed out in peacetime, but when skilled tradesmen refused to allow semi- or unskilled to work, it meant a serious slowing down of wartime production. Ernest Bevin (1881–1951), Minister of Labour in Churchill's coalition government, was horrified at what he regarded as betrayal and labelled Andrews' government as weak and vacillating.

Andrews' junior ministers and Unionist backbenchers urged him to show some positive signs of leadership. They reminded him of the Rev WA Watson's speech made on his appointment as Moderator of the Presbyterian Church in June 1941:

> After the big blitz of a few weeks ago, I was inexpressibly shocked at the wrecked houses and shops but I was more inexpressibly shocked at the sight of the people I saw walking the streets. I have been working nineteen years in Belfast and never saw the like of them before – wretched people, very undersized and underfed, down-and-out-looking men and women. They had been bombed out of their homes and were wandering the street. Is it creditable to us that there should be such people in a Christian country?... If something is not done now to remedy this rank inequality, there will be a revolution after the war.

This prophetic sermon was all the more effective because of its provenance and the undoubted gravitas of the speaker. The steadily growing opposition asked for a statement of post-war plans and details of necessary reforms but all Andrews could manage were polite meaningless words. It was the damning report of atrocious living conditions in the Belfast slums, called by one MP (also a doctor) 'the slaughter of the innocents', that finally forced his hand. On 1 October 1942 the Corporation was suspended *sine die* and commissioners, led by CW Grant, a civil servant, were appointed to run the city. It was noted that Sir Crawford McCullagh, the Lord Mayor, retained his ceremonial robes and showed no reluctance to wearing them. This situation persisted for three and a half years but even this reluctant action was insufficient to save Andrews. He was urged to purge if not actually remove his old cabinet, but as before, he vacillated. Faced with an ultimatum from an increasingly rebellious Parliamentary party on 19 January 1943 to give at least an indication of reform, he proposed no immediate action again; there could be no changes until after Easter.

Easter Sunday in that year fell on the latest possible date, 25 April, reckoned simply as the first Sunday after the first full moon after the vernal equinox. Three days later on Wednesday, 28 April, Andrews was ousted. Any promises he had made at Stormont for a new caring regime after the war were vague and unconvincing. His ineptitude as a leader in war gave no confidence in him as a social reformer in time of peace. The leader of his critics was Sir Basil Brooke, who rather than seem any kind of initiator of a *coup d'état*, had with others drawn up a number of proposals that were presented to Andrews. When he rejected these without discussion he was forced to resign and Brooke became prime minister on 1 May. Brooke's reshuffle was all but absolute; he and MacDermott, now Attorney-General, were the only survivors from Andrews' team. Nationalists had no regrets about the eclipse of Bates but they were offended that Midgley, a noted anti-Catholic, got MacDermott's post as Minister of Public Security. Brooke was more industrious and intelligent than Andrews but he was, if anything, more hardline in his Unionism. As a strong supporter of the Orange Order and commandant of the Fermanagh B-Specials he was certain of nationalists' 'disloyal' intentions and would broke no amelioration of their situation.

Though he brought the war economy up to scratch and successfully delivered the British welfare state legislation of the Labour government of Clement Attlee (1883–1967), his animus against northern nationalists caused his government later to object to family allowances being given to the younger children of large families. The reason advanced was fiscal probity, and there was no suggestion that its main impetus was against Catholics. They were, however, believed with some statistical evidence to be the main beneficiaries of the system. Westminster, however, insisted that the 'step-by-step' policy should be maintained. After the Blitz there was some lessening of sectarianism because of shared misery and a casualty list that more or less reflected the 3:1 ratio of creed. True, a majority of the churches that sustained serious damage were Protestant: nineteen Presbyterian, twelve Church of Ireland, eight Methodist, but in a city famous for Sabbath worship the Protestant churches greatly outnumbered the Catholic ones anyway. In an odd kind of 'fair trade' balance to this, of public elementary schools (as primary schools were known then) completely destroyed during the raids, six out of ten were Catholic, as were twelve out of twenty-nine requiring major repairs. Logic plays little part in visceral sectarianism. The shutter-down attitude of Brooke and his cabinet to the rights of the one-third nationalist population for the next twenty years was one of the contributory factors of the later troubles and the long attrition that wounded the city far more, and caused its citizens greater grief, than the spring Luftwaffe air raids. Though it is easy optimistically to overstate the détente between Northern Ireland's besetting curse of tribalism there were almost two and a half decades of low animosity when statesmanship rather than politics might have changed the whole tenor of life in the north in general and Belfast in particular.

The temper of the war against Germany was irrevocably changed after Barbarossa and Pearl Harbor but neither the terrified people of Belfast and Derry, nor their perplexed masters, had any idea of this. No further raids occurred and the excitement of the American forces in Northern Ireland tended to raise the spirits. Yet there was no doubt that the region remained a likely target, especially when the shipyards and plane factories (two-thirds of which had been destroyed) were repaired and enlarged, and reached full capacity. To prevent another raid that might totally shut down work again individual minor aspects of the construction of planes and ships were undertaken at dispersed locations scattered throughout the city and environs. It was after the raids that Belfast people first felt themselves engaged fully in the fight, a real part of the war effort, against Hitler and his Nazis. This in spite of the automatic pieties of Unionist politicians.

Even nationalists, hitherto instinctively wary of positive involvement, took more part in civil defence, encouraged by some Church leaders. Their distrust of Unionism, if not individual Unionists, and their atavistic suspicion of Britain were at its lowest level since the founding of the partial state. The planes made in Shorts – Herefords, Stirlings, Bombays and even Sunderlands – played a significant part in 'terror' raids, as they were later called, directed against the civilian population of German cities. One firm in Alfred

Street, close to the city centre, made particularly lethal incendiary devices call the 'jettisonable tanks', the main source of the fire-storms that set Hamburg alight and killed up to 135,000 civilians in Dresden in seventy minutes on the night of 13–14 February 1945.

As the city slowly emerged from its pathological bewilderment and terror the authorities, military and civil, began to mend the dykes. During the raids and the aftermath, serving soldiers stationed in or near the city had been active in rescue and clear-up. Their advice was useful in the defence and welfare reforms that were seen to be necessary. Extra equipment and fire-fighting personnel begged from the War Office had arrived as early as the Friday of Easter Week and now they were stationed at appropriate defensive points. More searchlights, ack-ack and a squadron of Defiant P82 night fighters, famous for their trick of attacking Luftwaffe bombers from beneath, and known as 'Daffies' to their irreverent pilots, were sent to Northern Ireland. More day fighters, Spitfires and Hurries (as the smaller planes were affectionately called), reinforced the squadron based at RAF Aldergrove and a more serviceable network of radar stations with more reliable connections with the centre at Prestwick was established. The steel plates for Morrison table shelters had been dispatched early in May 1941 but it took months for the necessary bolts to arrive. The dispersal of manufacturing shops and sub-stores by the large firms was replicated by the government and civil service. Offices and whole departments were located in country areas, none, it must be admitted, anywhere west of the Bann.

The other fields of reform were in the fire-fighting service and refugee care. The 'Fire Raid' in particular had laid bare great inadequacies in fire-watching and fire-quenching. Equipment came in fits and starts from Britain; there were many more pumps available and the EWS static water tanks assured the availability of water should the mains suffer the same fractures as in the earlier raids. One of the breakdowns in service had been caused by an apparently deliberate refusal on the part of the senior city fire officers to amalgamate with the undoubtedly less trained AFS. The personnel of both services had shown sterling examples of individual heroism but there was an inevitable clash of command and direction. After a drive for recruitment in the AFS that increased its manpower by 2,190 full-time and 2,300 part-time members, it was subsumed into a National Fire Service (NFS) which linked all the local brigades throughout Northern Ireland from 1 April 1942. Training was intensified and the result was a scientifically trained force. Though it was never called upon to deal with such an intensive bombardment again it became the basis for the Northern Ireland Fire and Rescue Service that was to be employed on a nightly basis during the 1970s and 1980s. Fire-watching in business premises, public buildings and churches was adequate since it was made the responsibility of owners and managements, though it proved impossible to appoint reliable street fire-watchers to all vulnerable parts of the city, despite there being many volunteers, attracted by the offer of stirrup-pumps.

The provision of reception centres was rationalised with Belfast and Derry given 'first-line', 'second-line' and 'dispersal' rest centres, arranged in a series of concentric bands around the two cities, the ones nearer to the centre given greatest priority. The plan was coordinated by the WHC (Welfare Headquarters Control) and food, medicine and bedding were stored in case of more than temporary need. During the winter of 1941–42 the WHC established sixteen emergency camps, seventeen nursery centres, requisitioning schools, church halls, boy-scouts centres as required. Large buildings not already used by the armed forces were prepared as evacuee hostels. Typical of this requisitioning was the Slieve Donard Hotel in Newcastle, County Down, allowed to continue in its original function only with severe limitations. It is thankfully impossible to estimate how these new measures might have coped should the hell of the fiery spring of 1941 have been repeated but the lesson had been learned. Future generations have observed an element of stable door bolting about all these measures but people could not be sure that the horse thieves might not come again.

The blackout gave way to the dim-out and with the chance of invasion nil, the silenced church bells, the intended signal of German landings, were heard again. The war in the Atlantic was won and, as the spring of 1945 recovered from the vicious winter war, shortages eased. Young children who had never seen bananas but had heard them praised by older siblings declared themselves to be disappointed. The less popular dark chocolate was replaced not by the lush milk variety of peacetime but by a kind of halfway house called 'blended'. Soon the rubbery silk material that had been the skin of the obsolete barrage balloons began to be seen as material for handbags and school satchels. The GIs left taking with them the exotic extras that had eased wartime restrictions. People smoked Players, Woodbine and Gallaher's cigarettes again when they could get them. Camel, Lucky Strike and Philip Morris were part of a lost dream and even the Canadian Sweet Caporal were no longer available. In Derry forty U-boats surrendered by the skippers were docked at Lisahally and hundreds of bicycles provided for the American forces were bull-dozed into fragments. They had been offered at a peppercorn fee to the City Corporation but the offer was glacially refused. Things were back to normal!

Demobbed service men came home to find families rather different from those they left behind and vaguely discontented at getting their old jobs back. The space left in Messines Park became a weedy patch until new houses were built, and in Belfast the incongruous open spaces were a reminder of the terror of four years earlier. The austerity of post-war society and the painful birth of the welfare state meant that years would pass before the fissures were sealed. Attlee's landslide electoral victory was not replicated in Northern Ireland. A general election held on 14 June 1945 produced the following results: Unionists, 33; Independent Unionists, 2; Nationalists, 10; Labour, 2; Independent Labour, 1; Commonwealth Labour, 1; Socialist Republican, 1; Independents, 2. As the psephologists of the time might have said, 'No change there!' Belfast people, like those throughout the United Kingdom, were delighted with free education up to third-level, child benefit, and access to free dental treatment and oculist services. New teeth and spectacles became for a while a constant topic of conversation. The 'submerged tenth' seemed to benefit most from the new welfare system but then they needed it most. For years they had lived, at its politest, an occluded life and they had suffered most in the peripheral *Blitzkrieg*.

On a worldwide scale Belfast's Luftwaffe visitation was slight; the two minor and two major raids in the open season of April–May 1941 stand no comparison with the incessant bombing of, say, Plymouth, or the nightly pounding of 'Hell-Fire-Corner' – the triangle of Kent centred at Dover that was within range of German ack-ack at Calais and saw the Battle of Britain fought and won in the perfect summer of 1940 – or even the East End of London. It is hardly mentioned, if at all, in the chronicle histories of World War II. Yet it still lives in personal memories and, like O'Rourk's noble fare, 'will ne'er be forgot by those who were there and those who were not'. It is the kind of searing event that makes its way into folk memory and gives the impression of having been also felt by those who could not possibly have experienced it. A death toll of not much less than 1,200 may seem slight but nearly a 1,000 of those died in five hours. It had a fleeting wisp of glory in the bravery displayed by individuals, and with the evidence of 100,000 frightened people deserting home and city, it brought the government and Corporation before the court of public opinion, accused of incompetence, not to say disdain, for those entrusted to their care.

Select Bibliography

Bardon, Jonathan. *A History of Ulster*. Belfast: 1992.

Barton, Brian. *The Blitz – Belfast in the War Years*. Belfast: 1989

——————. *Northern Ireland in the Second World War*. Belfast: 1995

Belfast Telegraph. *Bombs on Belfast*. 1941 (Facsimile pub 1984)

Blake, John W. *Northern Ireland in the Second World War*. Belfast: 1956

Doherty, James. *Post 381: The Memoirs of a Belfast Air Raid Warden*. Belfast: 1989

Fisk, Robert. *In Time of War*. London: 1983

Gallagher, Charles. *Acorns and Oak Leaves*. Derry: 1981

Gray, Tony. *Ireland This Century*. London: 1995

Heritage Library, Derry. *The War Years in Derry 1939–45*: 1996

McClure, Elaine. *Bodies in Our Backyard*. Lurgan: 1993

McFadden, Owen. *The Century Speaks: Ulster Voices*. Dublin: 1999

(ed.) Mercer, Derrik. *Chronicle of the Second World War*. London: 1990

Moore, Brian. *The Emperor of Ice Cream*. London: 1965

Redmond, Sean. *Belfast is Burning 1941*. Dublin: 2002

Wills, Clair. *That Neutral Island – A Cultural History of Ireland During the Second World War*. London: 2007

Wood, Ian S. *Ireland During the Second World War*. London: 2002